A LONGMAN LATIN READER

SELECTIONS FROM OVID'S METAMORPHOSES

Baucis and Philemon
Acis, Galatea, and Polyphemus
Narcissus and Echo
Pentheus

Prepared by William S. Anderson and Mary Purnell Frederick

LONGMAN

Selections from Ovid's Metamorphoses

Longman, 10 Bank Street, White Plains, N.Y. 10606

Associated companies:
Longman Group Ltd., London
Longman Cheshire Pty., Melbourne
Longman Paul Pty., Auckland
Copp Clark Pitman, Toronto
Pitman Publishing Inc., New York

Authors: **Professor William S. Anderson**, University of California, Berkeley, California
Mary Purnell Frederick, The Head-Royce School, Oakland, California
Series Editor: **Professor Gilbert Lawall**, University of Massachusetts, Amherst, Massachusetts
Consultants: **Jane Harriman Hall**, Mary Washington College, Alexandria, Virginia
Richard A. LaFleur, University of Georgia, Athens, Georgia
Robert E. Morse, Saint Andrew's School, Boca Raton, Florida

Executive editor: Lyn McLean
Production editor: Elsa van Bergen
Text and cover designer: Gayle Jaeger
Production supervisor: Judith Stern

ISBN 0-582-36748-4

25 26 27 28 29 -V036- 13 12 11 10 09

CONTENTS

ACKNOWLEDGMENTS

This book is based in part upon materials for teaching these episodes from Ovid's *Metamorphoses* prepared by the following graduate students in the MAT Program in Latin and Classical Humanities at the University of Massachusetts at Amherst as partial fulfillment of the requirements for Latin 608, Teaching Latin Literature, taught by Professor Gilbert Lawall in spring semester, 1984: Sara M. Adkins, Brian Francis Duffy, Sara Honig, Claire Mazzola, John R. McVey, James Meyer, Michael W. Muchmore, Barbara Romaine, Sean Smith, Susan P. Twitchell, and Jean Waddell.

CREDITS

INTRODUCTION

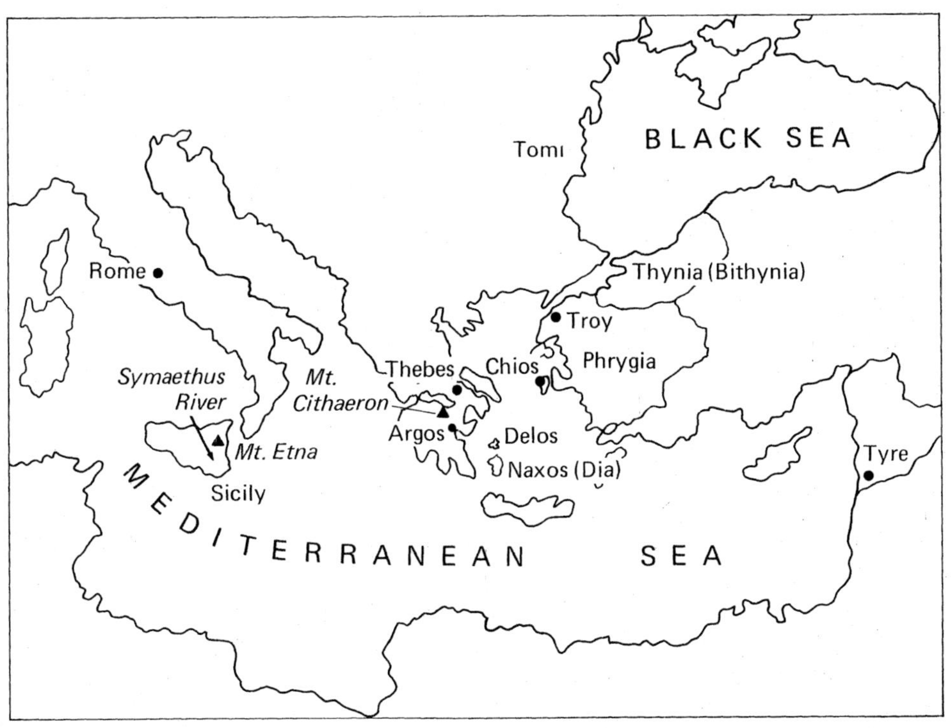

OVID'S LIFE AND WORKS

Ovid was born in 43 B.C. at the beginning of the last of Rome's civil wars, conflicts which had already continued on and off for almost a century. During these years the government of Rome had ceased to function constitutionally. The government, which modern historians call the Republic (**rēs pūblica**), had its power vested chiefly in a Senate or council of elder statesmen from aristocratic families, but also in popular assemblies and a variety of elected magistrates, especially two annually elected consuls. During the "century of revolution" (133–31 B.C.), however, real power was often in the hands of generals, who used their armies first against Rome's enemies but then against their own rivals. The last and most famous of these generals was Julius Caesar, who, shortly after he became dictator, was assassinated by a group of senators in 44 B.C., the year before Ovid was born. Caesar's followers and enemies struggled until 31 B.C., when Caesar's great-nephew and adopted son, Octavian, defeated his last rivals, Antony and Cleopatra, and emerged as the new leader of the Roman state. Thus, although Ovid lived several days' journey from Rome in the relative security of the countryside, he passed his early years in a period of extreme political instability.

Octavian, or Augustus as he came to be known from the title conferred on him in 27 B.C., ruled Rome for nearly forty-five years (30 B.C.–A.D. 14). After so many decades of strife, he brought a thorough peace to Rome's vast Empire (the lands encircling the Mediterranean, as well as southern Europe); he also restored it in other ways, such as by rebuilding temples and encouraging religious observances, and by passing laws designed to stabilize marriage and discourage childlessness. Most important, he restored constitutional government. Once again the Senate convened and deliberated, the assemblies met, and magistrates were elected. Nevertheless, we call this government that evolved under Augustus the Principate, not the Republic. Augustus, the "First Citizen" (**prīnceps**), maintained his authority by keeping control of the army and by securing collective powers that had been distributed among several magistrates during the Republic. Though his usual exercise of power was tactful, he could act absolutely when he thought it necessary, as when he banished for life his own daughter Julia on charges of adultery (2 B.C.). Ovid, too, was to feel his power.

When Ovid was about 17, his father sent him to Rome to study oratory, or public speaking, which was the ancient equivalent of law school and the usual preparation for a public or legal career. He soon rejected this career, however, choosing instead to become a poet. His principal topics were love and stories from mythology, his manner of dealing with them lighthearted, amusing, and occasionally satirical. His major works are the *Amores*, three books of love poems; the *Heroides*, verse letters from legendary women to absent husbands or lovers; and the *Ars amatoria*, in which Ovid poses as a learned expert, giving rules on the "art" of lovemaking. By his mid-40s Ovid was Rome's most popular poet. In A.D. 8, however, just as he was finishing the *Metamorphoses*, Augustus exiled him without warning to Tomi, a small, semi-barbarous town on the Black Sea in the northeastern corner of the Empire (modern Costanza in Romania), a place as unlike Rome and all its attractions as one could imagine. Ovid continued to write poetry for the last ten years of his life, but his exile at Tomi, without wife, friends, or civilized comforts, was extremely lonely and unhappy.

We do not know why Ovid was banished, and it is unlikely that adequate new evidence will ever surface to explain the mystery. There was probably some specific action, offensive to Augustus; in the poems written in exile he refers to a **carmen** (the *Ars amatoria*) and some indiscretion or mistake (**error**). In addition, it is hard to believe that Augustus, with his concern to renew the "old values" of Rome—commitment to the gods, to the state, and to the family—would have appreciated the themes of Ovid's poetry. The Princeps preferred Vergil and Horace, who had almost the status of court poets and who each at one time or another wrote poems that extolled the virtues of the new order and its author. Their poetry is generally more serious and frequently more concerned with public issues such as piety and loyalty. Ovid's poetry, with its lightness, its romance, its interest in human emotions as being important in themselves, and its eroticism, refers to a different kind of world.

THE *METAMORPHOSES*

The *Metamorphoses* are like Ovid's earlier poetry in theme but unlike it in meter and structure. They too are much about love and the stories from mythology, but the extent of the poem (almost 12,000 lines) and the meter Ovid chose (dactylic hexameter) show that he was placing himself in the tradition of epic poetry. (Ovid wrote all his earlier poetry in elegiac couplets, a meter consisting of alternating dactylic hexameters and pentameters.) The earliest epics in this tradition were composed around 800 B.C., in Greek, by Homer. Ovid takes the story of Polyphemus from one of these epics, the *Odyssey*, a story of one man's extraordinary travels and homecoming after the Trojan war. The other Homeric epic, the *Iliad*, is the story of one episode during that war. The first Latin poet to imitate the Greek epic in Latin dactyls was Ennius (early second century B.C.), who wrote an epic history of Rome, the *Annales*, from the fall of Troy down to his own time. The *De rerum natura* of Lucretius (95–55 B.C.) is a philosophical epic, an attempt to explain the physical laws of the universe. The most enduring and influential of the Latin epics, and the one in whose shadow Ovid would have felt himself writing, is the *Aeneid* of Vergil (70–19 B.C.); it describes the founding of Rome through the career of one exceptional man, Aeneas. What each of these poems shares, in spite of their difference in subject matter, is a seriousness of intent, and so if Ovid wrote in the epic meter, we may assume that, however delightful, amusing, or sometimes even ludicrous his stories may seem, there is also an underlying seriousness in his poem. (And similarly, in the serious stories, the reader will find unexpected comic moments.)

Metamorphosis is the Greek word for transformation (the title of Ovid's poem, *Metamorphoses*, is the plural form of the word), and all the hundreds of tales in the poem include some sort of transformation of men and women into animals, trees, rocks, birds, springs, flowers, constellations, or other natural objects. The framework for these tales is a chronological unfolding of world history from chaos in the beginning down to the murder of Julius Caesar and the projected metamorphosis of Augustus into a god. The connections among the stories are loose and unobtrusive, as from that of Narcissus to that of Pentheus (see page 57). Besides the motifs of transformation and love, what also unites the poem is Ovid's tone. (Tone in poetry is the speaker's or writer's attitude toward his subject, his audience, or himself; it is analogous to tone of voice in speaking and lets us understand the emotional coloring of a statement. Adjectives such as "amused," "serious," "sorrowful," "reverential," and "ironic" describe tone.) Ovid's tone is never simple: a sophisticated, witty, amusing reporter of the human scene, he can at the same time be serious and sensitive to profound human emotions. The story of Pygmalion, for example, is about a sculptor whose creation—an ivory statue of a young woman—is so beautiful that he falls in love with it; Venus rewards his passion by bringing the statue to life for him. Stated thus simply it is a sweet story, and Pygmalion's affection is endearing. Nevertheless, there are some potentially silly moments in the story when Pygmalion dresses the statue up and brings it presents; we are aware of Ovid lightly mocking the artist's potential to be so exclusively enamored of his own work.

The four selections from the *Metamorphoses* included in this book and printed with the line numbering of the Latin source are (1) Baucis and Philemon; (2) Acis, Galatea, and Polyphemus; (3) Narcissus and Echo; and (4) Pentheus. The stories are arranged with the shortest ones first. The theme of transformation is of course common to all the stories, and it will be interesting to compare the different metamorphoses, to examine who changes to what, and why. There are other motifs as well that two or more tales share. As we might expect from a poet who had already written many books of love poetry, love, in several different forms, is a frequent theme: married love, romantic love, self-love, unrequited love. Man's relationship with the gods (frequently his conflict with the gods) is also an issue. Since the will of the gods was believed to be expressed through oracles, prophecies too are found in three of the stories. A structural similarity to look for in all the stories is ring-structure: each story begins with a speech (such as by an oracle) or a setting or a particular Latin phrase, which returns at the end of the story. The "ring" around the story is one way the poet gives shape to his narrative; the repetition and return also remind the reader to review and judge what has happened during the story's course.

OVID'S STYLE

Attention to a few grammatical and stylistic habits of Ovid will make reading his poetry easier:

1. For the purposes of meter, Ovid typically substitutes the poetic ending **-ēre** for **-ērunt** in the perfect tense. After the first few instances this substitution will not be explained in the notes.
2. Because of the compressed quality of poetry, Ovid may omit a preposition. For example, **riguō collēgerat hortō** = **collēgerat ex** (or **in**) **riguō hortō.**
3. Although words in poetry do not always follow the usual prose order, Ovid does use arrangement of words to create phrases, and modifiers are rarely far away. A noun-adjective grouping may be bisected by a verb or participle, but the result is a close relationship between the verb or participle and the noun-adjective group. For example:

   riguō collēgerat hortō
   he had picked from the well-watered garden

   nōn acrī leviter versāta favillā
   lightly turned in a not-hot ash

4. Ovid, like other Latin poets, frequently uses a plural where we would, according to our logic, expect a singular. For example:

   vestra relinquite tēcta
   leave your house (lit., *leave your roofs*)

   levat illa . . . sordida terga suis

she lifts up the sooty side of bacon (lit., *the sooty backs*)

turpis equus, nisi colla iubae flāventia vēlent

a horse is shameful, if the mane does not cover his yellow neck (lit., *if the manes do not cover his yellow necks*)

5. The most frequent conjunction is **-que**. See, for example, Baucis II, "Hospitable Preparations," 635–652, where in seventeen and a half lines it occurs twelve times and is attached to verbs, participles, a preposition, nouns, adjectives, a relative pronoun, and an infinitive. (In the same passage the conjunction **et** occurs only four times.) The prevalence of this conjunction helps create a loosely structured, freely flowing narrative.
6. As to tenses, the narrative is carried along mainly in the perfect or vivid present, with background details being supplied by the pluperfect. For example, in Acis II, "A Prophecy Ignored," one necessary detail, about the soothsayer's prior experience, appears in a pluperfect (**fefellerat**); the remainder of the discussion between Polyphemus and the soothsayer and the description of the giant's subsequent actions are in either the present or the perfect. (The soothsayer's prophecy, however, is of course in the future: **rapiet**.)

PASSAGES FOR COMPARISON

The comparative readings that follow the Latin texts include selections from other works of literature that are either sources for these four tales from the *Metamorphoses* or analogous to them or later adaptations of them. For example, for the story of Baucis and Philemon, the selection is an analogous tale from Genesis, Chapters 18 and 19. Ovid is unlikely to have known the Old Testament, the sacred text of a minor sect in the Empire, even though it had been translated into Greek in the third century B.C. He did, however, make use of stories from Near Eastern legend which had been brought into Latin by way of the eastern Greeks. The story of Deucalion and Pyrrha, for example, sole survivors of a heaven-sent catastrophic flood, is analogous to another Near Eastern story, that of Noah. For the story of Acis, Galatea, and Polyphemus, the sources are given: extracts from the *Odyssey* and from a poem by Theocritus, a Sicilian Greek who wrote during the mid-third century B.C. For his characterization of Polyphemus, Ovid has taken details from these two very different versions of the giant cyclops. An instance of a later adaptation is Guillaume de Lorris' thirteenth-century retelling of the story of Narcissus.

READING ALOUD

To get the fullest appreciation of Ovid's poetry, your teacher will want you to learn a number of metrical rules so that you can scan (i.e., divide) the Latin line into syllables and feet. At first exposure these rules may seem to interfere with, rather than augment, the pleasure you can derive from reading Latin poetry. It is, of course, possible to read Latin poetry while remaining deaf to its meter, but to do so is to have only a partial experience of it. The sound of poetry is an important constituent, and in ancient poetry it was perhaps even more important because poetry was always read aloud, even if the reader was alone. (To read any written matter silently to oneself was considered freakish in antiquity. Caesar was once challenged in a meeting of the Senate because he read silently a personal message that had been delivered to him there.) Meter, not rhyme and accent, provided the primary shape to poetry, and so to recapture that shape we must try always to hear the bumpety-bumpety that carries hexameter verse along. It is a good habit to scan a few lines in every passage and to try to read the whole passage aloud according to the meter.

Ovid's *Metamorphoses* are a good introduction to classical Latin poetry. The narrative moves quickly, the characters and their settings are interesting, and Ovid's point of view is sympathetic. Because he writes, not about the state or ancient politics, but about people caught in familiar or plausible situations, we cannot help being carried along.

LIST OF POETIC TERMS

Throughout the notes and questions accompanying each section you will be introduced to a number of poetic terms. They will be defined at their first occurrence. The line references for these first occurrences are given below.

alliteration: Narcissus (414)
allusion: Acis, Galatea, and Polyphemus (760 and 769)
anaphora: Acis, Galatea, and Polyphemus (764–766)
antonomasia: Narcissus (437)
apostrophize: Narcissus and Echo (432)
chiastic: Pentheus (655)
epithet: Baucis and Philemon (627)
irony: Baucis and Philemon (668–669); Acis, Galatea, and Polyphemus (775)
metaphor: Acis (868–869)
metonomy: Baucis and Philemon (724)
patronymic: Baucis and Philemon (627)
simile: Acis, Galatea, and Polyphemus (851–852)
symbol: Acis, Galatea, and Polyphemus (784)
tone: Baucis and Philemon (684–685)
zeugma: Pentheus (645)

BAUCIS AND PHILEMON

The "Temple of Fortuna Virilis," Rome. Dating from the second century B.C., this little temple, which would have seemed old-fashioned in Ovid's time, may be imagined to be like the one into which Baucis and Philemon's hut evolved. Note the steps leading up.

616 ***obstipēscō, obstipēscere** (3), **obstipuī,** to be struck dumb, be stunned. **obstipuēre:** = **obstipuērunt.** Ovid frequently uses **-ēre** for **-ērunt.**
***tālis, -is, -e,** of such a character or kind (referring to what follows).
probārunt: = **probāvērunt**. Ovid frequently uses **-ārunt** for **-āvērunt.**
617 ***aevum, -ī** (*n*), age, length of years. **animō** and **aevō:** ablative of specification.
618 ***āiō, ais, ait, āiunt** (*defective*), to say.
***potentia, -ae** (*f*), power, influence, rule. Subject of **est** and **habet** (619).
***caelum, -ī** (*n*), sky, (here) the gods.
619 ***quisquis, quaequae, quidquid (quicquid),** whoever, whatever.
***superus, -a, -um,** above, higher, (plural) the gods above.
peragō, peragere (3), **perēgī, perāctum,** to carry through, complete.
620 **Quōque:** = **Et quō (quō** = **ut):** "And in order that. . . ."
dubitēs: Lelex uses the singular to aim his remarks at Pirithous. Why is this verb in the subjunctive?
tilia, -ae (*f*), linden (a kind of tree).
conterminus, -a, -um (+*dat.*), adjacent, near. ***quercus, -ūs** (*f*), oak.
621 **Phrygius, -a, -um,** Phrygian. Phrygia was the country that occupied central and western Asia Minor. **collibus** . . . **Phrygiīs:** supply **in**.
622 **Pelopēius, -a, -um,** Pelopeian, relating to Pelops, the king of Phrygia, or his descendants.
Pittheus, -eī (*m*), king of Troezen, a city in the northeast Peloponnesus (he is Pelops' son and Theseus' grandfather). Remember that Theseus is also listening to the story.
623 ***arvum, -ī** (*n*), ploughed field, (plural) territory, country. ***quondam,** formerly.
***rēgnō** (1), to reign. ***parēns, parentis** (*m*), parent, ancestor. **parentī**: dative of agent.
624 ***haud,** not. **hinc,** from here. **stagnum, -ī** (*n*), pool, lake.
***tellūs, tellūris** (*f*), ground, earth. **ōlim,** formerly, previously, once.
625 **celeber, celebris, celebre,** busy, populous, crowded.
mergus, -ī (*m*), seabird, gull. **mergīs**: ablative of means. **fulica, -ae** (*f*), waterfowl, coot.
***paluster, palustris, palustre,** marshy, swampy. ***unda, -ae** (*f*), wave.
626 ***Iuppiter, Iovis** (*m*), Jupiter, supreme god among the Romans. **speciē mortālī**: ablative of manner.
627 **vēnit:** take **Iuppiter** also as the subject.
Atlantiadēs, Atlantiadae (*m*), a descendant of Atlas, here Mercury, his grandson. Ovid identifies Mercury by his *patronymic,* a name derived from a paternal ancestor; **-adēs** (or **-idēs**) is a suffix meaning "the son or descendant of."
cādūcifer, cādūciferī (*m*), the staff-bearer. This *epithet,* invented by Ovid, refers to Mercury's caduceus or special staff. Epithets, which are common in ancient poetry, are fixed words or phrases that accompany a name as further identification.
āla, -ae (*f*), wing. **positīs** . . . **ālīs**: ablative absolute.
628 ***adeō, adīre** (*irreg.*), **adiī, aditum,** to approach. **adiēre**: see note on **obstipuēre** (616).
***requiēs, requiētis** (*f*), rest, repose. **requiem:** the usual accusative singular form.
locum requiemque: in English we would turn one of these nouns into an adjective or prepositional phrase for a more idiomatic expression.
629 **sera, -ae** (*f*), bolt, bar (of a door).
ūna: what noun, understood, does this adjective modify?
***recipiō, recipere** (3), **recēpī, receptum,** to receive, welcome.
630 **stipula, -ae** (*f*), stalk, straw. ***canna, -ae** (*f*), reed.
631 **pius, -a, -um,** dutiful, faithful, devout, loyal.
***Baucis, Baucidis** (*f*), the wife of Philemon. ***anus, -ūs** (*f*), old woman.
parilis, -is, -e, similar, equal. **parilī** . . . **aetāte**: ablative of description.
***Philēmōn, Philēmonis** (*m*), the husband of Baucis.
632 **Illā** . . . **illā**: with **casā** (633).
***iuvenālis, -is, -e,** youthful, young. **annīs** . . . **iuvenālibus**: ablative of time when.
633 **cōnsenēscō, cōnsenēscere** (3), **cōnsenuī,** to grow old.
***casa, -ae** (*f*), hut, cottage. **paupertās, paupertātis** (*f*), poverty.
***fateor, fatērī** (2), **fassus sum,** to accept as true, acknowledge. **fatendō** and **ferendō** (634): both take **paupertātem** as a direct object. Why are these gerunds in the ablative?
634 **levem**: to be taken after what verb? **nec inīquā** (= **et aequā) mente**: ablative of manner.

OVID, *METAMORPHOSES* VIII.616–724

I. *The Setting*

As the story opens, there has just been a burst of laughter. Over a lavish dinner, the river god Achelous, host to three travelers, has been telling how an island that they see from their dining couches was once a girl whom he loved, now metamorphosed by Neptune. Two of the travelers, Theseus and Lelex, are awed by this miracle; the third, young Pirithous, ridicules their belief in the power of the gods to transform appearances. Lelex responds to this challenge to piety by telling a tale of his own.

Obstipuēre omnēs nec tālia dicta probārunt,
ante omnēsque Lelex animō mātūrus et aevō
sīc ait: "Inmēnsa est fīnemque potentia caelī
nōn habet et, quidquid superī voluēre, perāctum est.
Quōque minus dubitēs, tiliae contermina quercus
collibus est Phrygiīs, mediō circumdata mūrō:
ipse locum vīdī; nam mē Pelopēia Pittheus
mīsit in arva suō quondam rēgnāta parentī.
Haud procul hinc stagnum est, tellūs habitābilis ōlim,
nunc celebrēs mergīs fulicīsque palustribus undae.
Iuppiter hūc speciē mortālī cumque parente
vēnit Atlantiadēs positīs cādūcifer ālīs;
mīlle domōs adiēre locum requiemque petentēs,
mīlle domōs clausēre serae; tamen ūna recēpit,
parva quidem stipulīs et cannā tēcta palustrī,
sed pia: Baucis anus parilīque aetāte Philēmōn
illā sunt annīs iunctī iuvenālibus, illā
cōnsenuēre casā paupertātemque fatendō
effēcēre levem nec inīquā mente ferendō.

1. **What truth does Lelex hope his story will prove?** (618–619)
2. **What features of the landscape does he mention?** (620–625) **Why do you think he does so?**
3. **What difficulty do the travelers have?** (628–629) **What were the rules of hospitality in the ancient world?**
4. **What contrast does the repetition in 628–629 emphasize? What other contrasts can you find in this tale?**
5. **What is the house like? What materials is it made of?** (630) **What does this information tell us about the inhabitants?**
6. **Who are the four characters in this tale, and what are their relationships?**
7. **What seems to be the central issue or problem in this story?**

635 **rēfert, rēferre** (*irreg.*), **rētulit,** it makes a difference.
*__dominus, -ī__ (*m*), master of a house, lord.
*__illīc__ (*adv.*), there. Read the line as **dominōsne illīc an famulōs requīrās. requīrās**: subjunctive with alternative indirect questions. *__famulus, -ī__ (*m*), servant, slave.
requīrō, requīrere (3), **requīsīvī (requīsiī), requīsītum,** to seek, inquire about.
637 *__ergō__, for that reason, therefore. **caelicola, -ae** (*m/f*), god or goddess.
*__Penātēs, Penātium__ (*m pl*), the gods of a Roman household (kept as images in the central hall or atrium), (by extension) one's home.
638 *__submittō, submittere__ (3), **submīsī, submissum,** to lower, bow (the head), bend (the knee). **submissō . . . vertice**: ablative absolute.
intrō (1), to go into, enter. **intrārunt:** = **intrāvērunt**.
vertex, verticis (*m*), crown of the head. **postis, postis** (*m*), doorpost, (plural) door.
639 *__membrum, -ī__ (*n*), limb. *__senex, senis__ (*m*) old man. **relevō** (1), to reduce the load of, lighten.
sedīle, sedīlis (*n*), seat, bench, chair. **positō . . . sedīlī**: ablative absolute.
640 **quō:** relative adverb referring to **sedīlī,** "upon which."
superiniciō, superinicere (3), **superiniēcī, superiniectum,** to throw on top.
textum, -ī (*n*), cloth, woven fabric. **rudis, -is, -e,** rough.
sēdulus, -a, -um, attentive, painstaking.
641 *__focus, -ī__ (*m*), hearth, fireplace. *__tepidus, -a, -um,__ warm.
cinis, cineris (*m*), ashes, embers.
dīmoveō, dīmovēre (2), **dīmōvī, dīmōtum,** to move aside, remove.
642 **suscitō** (1), to rouse, stir up, awaken. **hesternus, -a, -um,** yesterday's.
*__folium, -ī__ (*n*), leaf. **cortex, corticis** (*m/f*), bark. *__siccus, -a, -um,__ dry.
643 **nūtriō, nūtrīre** (4), **nūtrīvī (nūtriī), nūtrītum,** to nourish, feed.
*__flamma, -ae__ (*f*), flame. *__anima, -ae__ (*f*), breath.
prōdūcō, prōdūcere (3), **prōdūxī, prōductum,** to bring or draw forth.
anīlis, -is, -e, characteristic of an old woman, old woman's.
644 **multifidus, -a, -um,** split into many pieces, splintered.
fax, facis (*f*), torch, torch material.
rāmālia, rāmālium (*n pl*), branches, twigs. **āridus, -a, um,** dry.
*__tēctum, -ī__ (*n*), roof, ceiling. **tēctō**: ablative of place from which.
645 *__admoveō, admovēre__ (2), **admōvī, admōtum** (+ *dat.*), to move (something) near, apply to (something.)
aēnum, -ī (*n*), bronze or copper pot.
646 **quod**: the antecedent is **holus** (647). *__coniunx, coniugis__ (*m/f*), spouse (husband or wife).
*__riguus, -a, -um,__ irrigated, well-watered. *__hortus, -ī__ (*m*), garden. **hortō**: supply **in**.
647 **truncō** (1), to lop, strip of branches or foliage. **holus, holeris** (*n*), vegetable, cabbage.
foliīs: ablative of separation. **furca, -ae** (*f*), fork.
*__levō__ (1), to lift, remove. **bicornis, -is, -e,** two-pronged.
648 **sordidus, -a, -um,** dirty, grimy, blackened.
terga: where English refers to a "side" of bacon, Latin calls it a "back."
*__sūs, suis__ (*m/f*), pig. *__niger, nigra, nigrum,__ black, dark-colored.
tignum, -ī (*n*), beam, plank, timber. **nigrō . . . tignō:** supply **dē**.
649 **resecō, resecāre** (1), **resecuī, resectum,** to cut back, cut off.
tergus, tergoris (*n*), the back of an animal (used for meat). Take **servātō . . . diū . . . dē tergore** together.
650 **secō, secāre** (1), **secuī, sectum,** to cut, carve, detach.
domō, domāre (1), **domuī, domitum,** to subdue, overcome, soften. **domat:** this verb usually refers to the taming of animals, the conquering of people by war, or the controlling of passions. What makes its use here comical?
ferveō, fervēre (2), **ferbuī,** to boil.
651 *__sermō, sermōnis__ (*m*), speech, talk.

II. *Hospitable Preparations*

As Lelex continues his tale, describing both the hut and the dinner preparations that Baucis and Philemon make for their guests, we learn more about the characters of the old people and their relationship, as well as about ancient rules of hospitality.

"Nec rēfert, dominōs illīc famulōsne requīrās:
tōta domus duo sunt, īdem pārentque iubentque.
Ergō ubi caelicolae parvōs tetigēre Penātēs
submissōque humilēs intrārunt vertice postēs,
membra senex positō iussit relevāre sedīlī,
quō superiniēcit textum rude sēdula Baucis,
inque focō tepidum cinerem dīmōvit et ignēs
suscitat hesternōs foliīsque et cortice siccō
nūtrit et ad flammās animā prōdūcit anīlī
multifidāsque facēs rāmāliaque ārida tēctō
dētulit et minuit parvōque admōvit aēnō,
quodque suus coniunx riguō collēgerat hortō,
truncat holus foliīs; furcā levat illa bicornī
sordida terga suis nigrō pendentia tignō
servātōque diū resecat dē tergore partem
exiguam sectamque domat ferventibus undīs.
Intereā mediās fallunt sermōnibus hōrās
sentīrīque moram prohibent.

1. **How extensive is Baucis and Philemon's household?** (635–636)
2. **How do the gods enter the house?** (637–638) **Why is this detail important?**
3. **How do Baucis and Philemon provide for the physical comfort of their guests?** (639–640)
4. **What actions show that Baucis is *sēdula*?** (640–645) **What are the old people preparing for dinner?** (646–650)
5. **Baucis and Philemon are described in the first part of the tale (631–634) as equals in age and alike in authority. How do their preparations for their guests reveal their equality or similarity?**
6. **How do the guests and hosts pass the time before dinner?** (651–652)

652 **alveus, -ī** (*m*), tub, trough.
653 **fāgineus, -a, -um,** of beechwood. **clāvus, -ī** (*m*), nail.
suspendō, suspendere (3), **suspendī, suspēnsum,** to hang, suspend.
ānsa, -ae (*f*), handle.
654 **artus, -ūs** (*m*), joint, part of the body, (here) foot.
foveō, fovēre (2), **fōvī, fōtum,** to warm, give physical ease to, soothe.
655 **torus, -ī** (*m*), mattress. ***mollis, -is, -e,** soft, loose, pliant. **ulva, -ae** (*f*), coarse grass.
656 **lectus, -ī** (*m*), bed, couch. **lectō**: dative with compound verb.
sponda, -ae (*f*), frame of a bed or couch. **spondā pedibusque salignīs**: ablatives of description.
***salignus, -a, -um,** made of willow wood.
657 ***vēlō** (1), to cover. ***fēstus, -a, -um,** festive, characteristic of a holiday.
658 **sternō, sternere** (3), **strāvī, strātum,** to lay out, spread, scatter, strew.
et: "even."
vīlis, -is, -e, cheap, worth little.
659 **lectō**: dative of agent with the gerundive **indignanda**.
indignor, indignārī (1), **indignātus sum,** to complain, protest, disdain. The gerundive of a deponent verb is passive in meaning, "to be disdained."
660 **accumbō, accumbere** (3), **accubuī, accubitum,** to recline at dinner.
***mēnsa, -ae** (*f*), table.
succinctus, -a, -um, having one's clothes tucked up under a belt to allow for freedom of movement.
***tremō, tremere** (3), **tremuī,** to tremble, quake.
661 **inpār, inparis,** unequal, uneven.
662 **testa, -ae** (*f*), potsherd, fragment of crockery.
quae: to what noun does this relative pronoun refer?
subdō, subdere (3), **subdidī, subditum,** to place under. ***clīvus, -ī** (*m*), slope, incline.
663 **tollō, tollere** (3), **sustulī, sublātum,** to raise, remove, eliminate.
aequātam: what noun must you supply?
menta, -ae (*f*), mint. **tergeō, tergēre** (2), **tersī, tersum,** to rub clean, wipe.
vireō, virēre (2), **viruī,** to be fresh and green.
664 **hīc,** here, in this place. **bicolor, bicolōris,** of two colors.
sincērus, -a, -um, unblemished, pure, virgin. **bāca, -ae** (*f*), olive.
Minerva, -ae (*f*), Roman goddess of handicrafts, equated with Athena, the Greek goddess of wisdom (the olive tree was sacred to both).
665 **condō, condere** (3), **condidī, conditum,** to preserve, bottle for keeping.
***cornum, -ī** (*n*), wild cherry. **faex, faecis** (*f*), dregs, wine-lees, sediment.
666 **intibum, -ī** (*n*), endive. **rādīx, rādīcis** (*f*), root, radish.
***lac, lactis** (*n*), milk. ***lac coāctum:** "cheese." **massa, -ae** (*f*), lump.
667 **ōvum, -ī** (*n*), egg. **versō** (1), to keep turning over.
favīlla, -ae (*f*), ashes of a fire.
668 **fictilis, fictilis** (*n*), earthenware, pottery. **fictilibus:** supply **in.**
***caelō** (1), to emboss, engrave.
669 ***sistō, sistere** (3), **stetī (stitī), statum,** to stand, set, place.
argentum, -ī (*n*), silver. What is the wine bowl really made of?
***crātēr, crātēris** (*m*) (*Greek loan word*), mixing bowl for wine.
fabricō (1), to fashion, construct. **fāgus, -ī** (*f*), beech (either the tree or its wood).
670 **pōculum, -ī** (*n*), cup. **quā**: "where." ***cavus, -a, -um,** hollow, concave, (here) porous.
***flāveō, flāvēre** (2), to be yellow. **inlinō, inlinere** (3), **inlēvī, inlitum,** to smear.
***cēra, -ae** (*f*), wax.

III. *Dining with the Gods*

The old people continue to make their guests welcome and to prepare dinner. At the last moment there is a small awkwardness with the table, but then the meal begins.

"Erat alveus illīc
fāgineus, dūrā clāvō suspēnsus ab ānsā:
is tepidīs inplētur aquīs artūsque fovendōs
accipit. In mediō torus est dē mollibus ulvīs
inpositus lectō spondā pedibusque salignīs.
Vestibus hunc vēlant, quās nōn nisi tempore fēstō
sternere cōnsuerant, sed et haec vīlisque vetusque
vestis erat lectō nōn indignanda salignō.
Accubuēre deī. Mēnsam succincta tremēnsque
pōnit anus, mēnsae sed erat pēs tertius inpār:
testa parem fēcit; quae postquam subdita clīvum
sustulit, aequātam mentae tersēre virentēs.
Pōnitur hīc bicolor sincērae bāca Minervae
conditaque in liquidā corna autumnālia faece
intibaque et rādīx et lactis massa coāctī
ōvaque nōn ācrī leviter versāta favīllā,
omnia fictilibus; post haec caelātus eōdem
sistitur argentō crātēr fabricātaque fāgō
pōcula, quā cava sunt, flāventibus inlita cērīs.

1. **What is the purpose of the beechwood trough?** (652–655)
2. **What do Baucis and Philemon provide for a dining couch?** (655–656) **What is noteworthy about its covering?** (657–659)
3. **Who of the four present eat dinner?** (660) **What does this detail reveal about the old couple's hospitality?**
4. **What is the difficulty with the table, and how is it solved?** (661–663) **What is the effect of mentioning this detail?**
5. **What foods are served as appetizers?** (664–667) **What does the next course consist of?** (668–670)
6. **What are the serving dishes and drinking cups made of?** (668–669) **In describing the bowl the wine is mixed in (*caelātus eōdem . . . argentō crātēr*), Ovid is using *irony*, a common poetic strategy, by which he can say one thing but mean something quite contrary. What is he saying and what does he mean? What is the point of this ironic statement?**
7. **The narrator has already mentioned Baucis and Philemon's poverty (633). What details can you find in this passage that reveal that they are poor?**
8. **How can you tell that Baucis and Philemon's preparations for dinner are not their customary ones? What does their behavior reveal about conventions of hospitality in the ancient world? What does it reveal about their characters?**

671 **epulae, -ārum** (*f pl*), feast, food fit for a banquet.
caleō, calēre (2), **caluī,** to be hot or warm.
672 ***vīnum, -ī** (*n*), wine.
***senecta, -ae** (*f*), old age. **longae . . . senectae:** what kind of genitive is this?
673 **mēnsa secunda**, dessert. **mēnsīs . . . secundīs:** dative of indirect object.
674 **nux, nucis** (*f*), nut.
***misceō, miscēre** (2), **miscuī, mixtum,** to mix, bring together.
rūgōsus, -a, -um, wrinkled.
cārica, -ae (*f*), dried fig.
***palma, -ae** (*f*), palm tree, date.
675 ***prūnum, -ī** (*n*), plum.
***patulus, -a, -um,** broad.
redoleō, redolēre (2), to give off a smell, be fragrant.
mālum, -ī (*n*), apple.
canistrum, -ī (*n*), food basket.
676 ***vītis, vītis** (*f*), grapevine.
***ūva, -ae** (*f*), bunch of grapes.
677 ***candidus, -a, -um,** white.
favus, -ī (*m*), honeycomb.
***vultus, -ūs** (*m*), face, countenance.
678 **iners, inertis,** lazy, sluggish.
***pauper, pauperis,** poor, meager, of little worth.
679 ***totiēns,** as often, so often.
***hauriō, haurīre** (4), **hausī (hauriī), haustum (haurītum),** to drink, empty out, consume.
crātēra: Greek accusative singular.
680 **vident:** who are the subjects of this verb?
succrēscō, succrēscere (3), **succrēvī,** to grow up from below, grow up as a replacement.
681 ***adtonitus, -a, -um,** stunned, stupefied, dazed.
***novitās, novitātis** (*f*), newness, surprise, strange phenomenon.
paveō, pavēre (2), to be frightened, be terrified.
supīnus, -a, -um, (of the hands) turned palm upwards.
682 **concipiō, concipere** (3), **concēpī, conceptum,** to conceive, produce, utter.
683 ***venia, -ae** (*f*), favor, kindness, allowance, excuse, pardon.
daps, dapis (*f*), feast, meal, banquet.
nūllīs . . . parātibus: dative with **veniam** (so also **dapibus**), lit., "pardon for the no preparations," i.e., "for their lack of preparation." Baucis and Philemon humbly assume that all they have done has not been enough.
684 ***ūnicus, -a, -um,** one and only, sole.
ānser, ānseris (*m*), goose.
vīlla, -ae (*f*), country house, farm.
685 ***dīs:** dative plural of **deus.**
***hospes, hospitis,** entertained as a guest.
mactō (1), to sacrifice.
686 ***penna, -ae** (*f*), feather, wing.
tardōs: supply **eōs.** To whom does this refer?
fatīgō (1), to tire out, weary, exhaust.
687 **ēlūdō, ēlūdere** (3), **ēlūsī, ēlūsum,** to deceive, escape from.
tandem, at last, finally.
688 **cōnfugiō, cōnfugere** (3), **cōnfūgī,** to flee (to a person or god) for protection.
cōnfūgisse: perfect infinitive used emphatically for the present.

IV. *Wine and a Goose*

After three more courses, the dinner comes to a sudden end with a startling event. The old people's response to this strange phenomenon reveals both their characters and their means.

"Parva mora est, epulāsque focī mīsēre calentēs,
nec longae rūrsus referuntur vīna senectae
dantque locum mēnsīs paulum sēducta secundīs.
Hīc nux, hīc mixta est rūgōsīs cārica palmīs
prūnaque et in patulīs redolentia māla canistrīs
et dē purpureīs collēctae vītibus ūvae;
candidus in mediō favus est: super omnia vultūs
accessēre bonī nec iners pauperque voluntās.
Intereā totiēns haustum crātēra replērī
sponte suā per sēque vident succrēscere vīna.
Adtonitī novitāte pavent manibusque supīnīs
concipiunt Baucisque precēs timidusque Philēmōn
et veniam dapibus nūllīsque parātibus ōrant.
Ūnicus ānser erat, minimae custōdia vīllae,
quem dīs hospitibus dominī mactāre parābant;
ille celer pennā tardōs aetāte fatīgat
ēlūditque diū tandemque est vīsus ad ipsōs
cōnfūgisse deōs.

1. **Is *epulās* (671) an appropriate word to describe the main course? (Review lines 645–650.) What does the dessert course consist of?** (674–677) **What is the course in between?** (672–673)
2. **The narrator describes the old couple's goodwill toward their guests as *nec . . . pauper* (678), as if the dinner itself has been poor. Has it?**
3. **What is the surprising behavior of the wine bowl?** (679–680) **How is it a fitting conclusion to the dinner?**
4. **What frightens the old people?** (681) **What do they pray for?** (682–683)
5. **What do they prepare to do to the goose?** (684–685) **Why? How is this little episode in keeping with the characters of Baucis and Philemon, as already established? What is the narrator's *tone* in describing it? Remember the definition of tone given in the Introduction: the speaker's or writer's attitude toward his subject, his audience, or himself.**
6. **What details about religious practice in ancient Rome does this episode reveal?**

688 ***vetō** (1), to forbid. **vetuēre necārī: vetō** takes an infinitive with subject accusative. What noun in the accusative case must you supply?
689 **que**: this is the enclitic **-que**, "and," and is to be taken with **dīxērunt** (690).
***luō, luere** (3), **luī**, to suffer (a punishment, **poenās**).
vīcīnia, -ae (*f*), neighborhood, neighbors.
690 **inmūnis, -is, -e** (+ *gen.*), free from, exempt from. **inmūnibus:** predicate dative after **esse** (691), agreeing with **vōbīs.**
691 **dabitur**: impersonal, "it will be granted."
692 **comitō** (1), to go along with, accompany.
***gradus, -ūs** (*m*), step, pace.
arduum, -ī (*n*), high place or situation.
693 **ambō, -ae, -ō** , both, both together.
***baculum, -ī** (*n*), walking stick.
694 ***nītor, nītī** (3), **nīxus sum,** to strain, struggle.
***vestīgium, -ī** (*n*), footprint, footstep.
695 **summō**: ablative of place from which.
semel, a single time, once.
696 ***flectō, flectere** (3), **flexī, flexum,** to bend, turn. **oculōs flectere,** to look behind one.
***mergō, mergere** (3), **mersī, mersum,** to sink, drown, flood.
697 ***prōspiciō, prōspicere** (3), **prōspexī, prōspectum,** to see before one.
tantum, only.
698 **dēfleō, dēflēre** (2), **dēflēvī, dēflētum,** to weep over.
***fātum, -ī** (*n*), destiny, fate, death, doom.
700 **furca, -ae** (*f*), fork, (here) Y-shaped pieces of wood used as the corner posts of the hut.
***subeō, subīre** (4), **subiī (subīvī), subitum,** to succeed to, replace.
701 **strāmen, strāminis** (*n*), straw, thatch.
flāvēscō, flāvēscere (3), to turn yellow, become golden.
adoperiō, adoperīre (4), **adoperuī, adopertum,** to cover over.
***marmor, marmoris** (*n*), marble.
702 ***foris, foris** (*f*), door.
aurō (1), to overlay with gold, gild.
703 **placidus, -a, -um,** kindly, indulgent, peaceful.
***Saturnius, -a, -um,** of Saturn, Saturn's. Since Jupiter is the son of Saturn, **Saturnius** is his patronymic. Compare **Atlantiadēs** (627).
***ēdō, ēdere** (3), **ēdidī, ēditum,** to give out, utter, proclaim.
***ōs, ōris** (*n*), mouth, lips, face.
704 **coniuge iustō:** why is this phrase in the ablative case?
705 **optō** (1), to wish for, desire, pray for. **optētis:** how do you explain this use of the subjunctive?
706 **iūdicium, -ī** (*n*), decision.

V. *Straw Into Gold*

Revealing themselves at last, the gods ask the old couple to make a different kind of sacrifice from the one they had intended, and then they explain why. Astonishing transformations follow.

"Superī vetuēre necārī,
'Dī,' que, 'sumus, meritāsque luet vīcīnia poenās
inpia,' dīxērunt; 'vōbīs inmūnibus huius
esse malī dabitur. Modo vestra relinquite tēcta
ac nostrōs comitāte gradūs et in ardua montis
īte simul!' Pārent ambō baculīsque levātī
nītuntur longō vestīgia pōnere clīvō.
Tantum aberant summō, quantum semel īre sagitta
missa potest: flexēre oculōs et mersa palūde
cētera prōspiciunt, tantum sua tēcta manēre.
Dumque ea mīrantur, dum dēflent fāta suōrum,
illa vetus dominīs etiam casa parva duōbus
vertitur in templum: furcās subiēre columnae,
strāmina flāvēscunt, adopertaque marmore tellūs
caelātaeque forēs aurātaque tēcta videntur.
Tālia tum placidō Sāturnius ēdidit ōre:
'Dīcite, iuste senex et fēmina coniuge iustō
digna, quid optētis!' Cum Baucide pauca locūtus
iūdicium superīs aperit commūne Philēmōn:

1. **What saves the goose?** (688)
2. **Who is to be punished and why?** (689–690) **(Review 626–630.) Who will be spared?** (690–691) **Is the punishment appropriate (*meritās*, 689)?**
3. **Where do the gods order Baucis and Philemon to go?** (691–693) **Is it an easy journey?** (693–694)
4. **Where do the old people pause?** (695–696) **What do they marvel at?** (696–698) **Where, earlier in the tale, has this swamp been described?**
5. **The phrase *mersa . . . cētera* (696–697) is opposed to *sua tēcta manēre* (697). What is included in the general word *cētera*? What does *suōrum* (698) refer to?**
6. **What is the difference between the gods' attitude toward the people of the neighborhood and that of Baucis and Philemon? What causes this difference?**
7. **Compare the metamorphosis of the hut (699–702) with that of the neighborhood houses (696–697). Which is more detailed? Why?**
8. **What is Jupiter's final command?** (704–705)
9. **How does Philemon reach his decision?** (705–706) **Is his course of action surprising or typical?**

707 **sacerdōs, sacerdōtis** (*m/f*), priest or priestess of a deity or temple.
dēlūbrum, -ī (*n*), temple, shrine.
708 ***concors, concordis,** like-minded, harmonious.
709 **auferō, auferre** (*irreg.*), **abstulī, ablātum,** to carry away, carry off.
auferat: explain this use of the subjunctive.
duōs: supply **nōs.**
710 **bustum, -ī** (*n*), funeral pyre, ashes, tomb. **busta**: poetic plural, to be translated as if singular.
tumulō (1), to cover with a burial mound.
711 ***vōtum, -ī** (*n*), a vow made to a god, prayer, desire, hope.
***fidēs, -eī** (*f*), fulfillment of a promise.
***tūtēla, -ae** (*f*), guardianship, protection. **tūtēla**: the abstract here represents the concrete, "the guardians."
712 **dōnec,** until, as long as, while.
***solvō, solvere** (3), **solvī, solūtum,** to loosen, weaken.
714 ***nārrō** (1), to relate, describe, tell.
***frondeō, frondēre** (2), to put forth leaves.
Philēmona: Greek accusative singular.
715 **senior, seniōris,** older.
716 ***super** (+ *acc.*), over, above, on top of.
***geminus, -a, -um,** twin, like, identical.
***crēscō, crēscere** (3), **crēvī, crētum,** to come into existence, arise, be born. **crēscente cacūmine**: ablative absolute.
***cacūmen, cacūminis** (*n*), peak, top.
717 **mūtuus, -a, -um,** mutual, reciprocal.
valē: "goodbye" (from **valeō**).
que: = **-que** (to be taken with **dīxēre** in line 718).
719 **frutex, fruticis** (*f*), shrub, stalk, shoot, (here) bark.
***adhūc,** up to the present time.
Thȳnēius, -a, -um, of Thynia (= Bithynia, a country on the Black Sea just north of Phrygia). Baucis and Philemon live in Phrygia (line 621), not Bithynia, but by association the narrator intends to refer to their country.
720 **incola, -ae** (*m/f*), inhabitant.
***truncus, -ī** (*m*), tree trunk.
721 ***vānus, -a, -um,** false, unreliable.
neque erat: supply in translation a noun such as "cause" or "reason." Syntactically, the indirect question is the predicate of **neque erat** (lit., "nor was there why they would wish. . . .").
722 **equidem** (*emphasizing an implied* **ego**), I for my part, personally speaking.
723 **serta, -ōrum** (*n pl*), chains of flowers, garlands.
***rāmus, -ī** (*m*), branch.
724 **Cūra deum (= deōrum):** the speaker uses *metonomy* to mean Baucis and Philemon, those who care for the gods. In metonomy one word is substituted for another to which it stands in close relationship—for example, the possessor for the thing possessed or the container for the thing contained. Here, the action stands for the actors. **sint** and **colantur**: jussive subjunctives.
***colō, colere** (3), **coluī, cultum,** to inhabit, look after, worship.

VI. *Guardians of the Temple*

Because of their special character and actions, Baucis and Philemon are granted two wishes. Lelex, at the conclusion of his story, explains how the old people ended their lives and what the meaning of their story is.

" 'Esse sacerdōtēs dēlūbraque vestra tuērī
poscimus, et quoniam concordēs ēgimus annōs,
auferat hōra duōs eadem, nec coniugis umquam
busta meae videam neu sim tumulandus ab illā.'
Vōta fidēs sequitur: templī tūtēla fuēre,
dōnec vīta data est; annīs aevōque solūtī
ante gradūs sacrōs cum stārent forte locīque
nārrārent cāsūs, frondēre Philēmona Baucis,
Baucida cōnspexit senior frondēre Philēmōn.
Iamque super geminōs crēscente cacūmine vultūs
mūtua, dum licuit, reddēbant dicta 'Valē' que
ō coniunx' dīxēre simul, simul abdita tēxit
ōra frutex: ostendit adhūc Thȳnēius illīc
incola dē geminō vīcīnōs corpore truncōs.
Haec mihi nōn vānī (neque erat, cūr fallere vellent)
nārrāvēre senēs; equidem pendentia vīdī
serta super rāmōs pōnēnsque recentia dīxī
'Cūra deum dī sint, et quī coluēre, colantur!' "

1. **What are Philemon's two requests?** (707–710) **Why do you think the couple makes these particular requests?**
2. **How long do Baucis and Philemon act as guardians of the temple?** (711–712)
3. **Where were they standing when their metamorphosis began?** (713) **Why is this detail important? What were they doing?** (713–714)
4. **Recount the stages of their metamorphosis.** (714–720) **What do they become? Is this change an answer to the wish expressed earlier?** (709–710) **Is it a fitting reward for their piety? Where, earlier in the tale, were we prepared for this change?**
5. **What does the speaker see as the moral of the tale?** (724) **Has his story proved its point? (Review 618–619.) Do you think he persuaded his audience?**
6. **What are Ovid's ideas about the gods? Why were Jupiter and Mercury traveling through Phrygia? Why were they in disguise?** (626–627) **Are their responses to what happens to them appropriate?**
7. **Ovid's style depends upon a curious mixture of serious and comic elements. Where in the story do you see such a mixture? What does the poet gain by using this approach?**
8. **The story of Baucis and Philemon (and their neighbors) is about piety, but it is told in the context of hospitality. The rewards for piety and the punishment for impiety in this context are great. Hospitality must therefore have been important in the ancient world. Why do you think it was?**

ACIS, GALATEA, AND POLYPHEMUS

"Odysseus Putting Out the Eye of the Cyclops Polyphemus," by Pellegrino Tibaldi, a Renaissance interpretation. Note the huge staff and pipe.

750 ***Ācis, Ācidis** (*m*), a son of Faunus.
Faunus, -ī (*m*), in Latin myth, the protecting deity of agriculture and shepherds; identified with the Greek Pan, he is represented in art with horns and goat's feet.
***nympha, -ae** (*f*), nymph, a semi-divine female spirit inhabiting woods, waters, etc.
Symaethis, Symaethidis (*f*), a daughter of the river-god Symaethus. The river Symaethus is in eastern Sicily, near Mt. Etna. **Faunō nymphāque Symaethide**: with **crētus**, ablatives of source without a preposition.
751 **voluptās, voluptātis** (*f*), pleasure, source of joy.
753 ***pulcher, pulchra, pulchrum,** beautiful, handsome.
octōnī, -ae, -a, eight each, occurring in groups of eight.
***iterum,** again, for the second time.
nātālis, nātālis (*m*), birthday. **octōnīs iterum** . . . **āctīs:** this phrase tells us how old Acis is.
754 **signō** (1), to mark. **signārat:** = **signāverat.**
***tener, tenera, tenerum,** tender, delicate, soft.
dubius, -a, -um, doubtful, uncertain, barely perceptible.
lānūgō, lānūginis (*f*), down. **māla, -ae** (f), cheek.
755 **hunc ego:** supply **petēbam.**
***Cyclōps, Cyclōpis** (*m*), one of the Cyclopes, one-eyed giant shepherds living on Sicily; this one is named Polyphemus (see 765). Ovid's audience would be familiar with this giant from Theocritus' *Idyll* XI and Homer's *Odyssey*. See "Passages for Comparison."
756 **quaesierīs:** perfect subjunctive (note the alternative **-īs** ending) in a future less vivid conditional sentence. The perfect subjunctive is used in this type of conditional sentence when the action of the if-clause is thought of as completed prior to the action of the main clause.
odium, -ī (n), hatred. **odium** . . . **amorne:** the **-ne** introduces the second alternative of a double indirect question. Translate, "(whether) hatred of the Cyclops *or* love of Acis was. . . ."
***amor, amōris** (*m*), love. **Cyclōpis** . . . **Ācidis** (757): why are these nouns in the genitive case?
758 **utrumque:** to what two nouns does this pronoun refer? With which does it agree in gender?
prō, oh.
759 ***Venus, Veneris** (*f*), in Latin myth the goddess of love, equated with the Greek Aphrodite.
almus, -a, -um, nurturing, kindly. **nempe,** of course, to be sure.
***inmītis, -is, -e,** harsh, merciless.
760 ***horreō, horrēre** (2), **horruī,** to shudder at, dread. **ipsīs** (759) . . . **silvīs:** dative with **horrendus.**
761 **inpūne,** without punishment, safely.
Olympus, -ī (*m*), the abode of the gods (sometimes located on a mountain, sometimes in the sky).
762 **sit:** explain this subjunctive.
cupīdō, cupīdinis (*m/f*), longing, desire.
763 ***ūrō, ūrere** (3), **ussī, ustum,** to burn, inflame.
oblīvīscor, oblīvīscī (3), **oblītus sum** (+ *gen.*), to forget. ***antrum, -ī** (*n*), cave, den.
764 **tibī** . . . **tibi:** note that the final *i* can be either long or short to fit the meter.
fōrmae . . . **placendī:** objective genitives with **cūra.**
765 **pectō, pectere** (3), **pexī (pexuī), pexum,** to comb.
rastrum, -ī (*n*), rake. ***Polyphēmus, -ī** (*m*), a Cyclops. ***capillus, -ī** (*m*), hair.
766 **libet, libēre** (2), **libuit (libitum est)** (*impersonal*), it is pleasing.
hirsūtus, -a, -um, hairy, shaggy. **falx, falcis** (*f*), sickle.
recīdō, recīdere (3), **recīdī, recīsum,** to cut back, prune.
***barba, -ae** (*f*), beard.
767 **conpōnō, conpōnere** (3), **conposuī, conpositum,** to arrange, compose.
768 **feritās, feritātis** (*f*), wildness, savagery.
***sitis, sitis** (*f*), thirst. ***cruor, cruōris** (*m*), blood, slaughter.
769 **cessō** (1), to cease, stop. ***carīna, -ae** (*f*), keel, hull, ship.

OVID, *METAMORPHOSES* XIII.750–898

I. *An Unhappy Triangle*

The setting for this story is a quiet corner beneath the waters of the sea, where two maidens, Scylla and Galatea, are exchanging confidences about love. Galatea is a sea nymph, the daughter of the sea gods Nereus and Doris. Scylla sympathetically wipes away Galatea's tears as Galatea tells her sad tale of lost love:

"Ācis erat, Faunō nymphāque Symaethide crētus,
magna quidem patrisque suī mātrisque voluptās,
nostra tamen maior; nam mē sibi iunxerat ūnī.
Pulcher et octōnīs iterum nātālibus āctīs
signārat tenerās dubiā lānūgine mālās:
hunc ego, mē Cyclōps nūllō cum fīne petēbat;
nec, sī quaesierīs odium Cyclōpis amorne
Ācidis in nōbīs fuerit praesentior, ēdam:
pār utrumque fuit. Prō quanta potentia rēgnī
est, Venus alma, tuī! Nempe ille inmītis et ipsīs
horrendus silvīs et vīsus ab hospite nūllō
inpūne et magnī cum dīs contemptor Olympī,
quid sit amor sēnsit nostrīque cupīdine captus
ūritur oblītus pecorum antrōrumque suōrum.
Iamque tibī fōrmae, iamque est tibi cūra placendī,
iam rigidōs pectis rastrīs, Polyphēme, capillōs,
iam libet hirsūtam tibi falce recīdere barbam
et spectāre ferōs in aquā et conpōnere vultūs;
caedis amor ferītāsque sitisque inmēnsa cruōris
cessant, et tūtae veniuntque abeuntque carīnae.

1. **What are the relationships among the three characters in the story? What is the central problem? From how many viewpoints could this story be told?**
2. **What is Acis' chronological age?** (753) **What else tells us how old he is?** (754)
3. **In Latin poetry the placement of words can visually reinforce meaning. How does the arrangement of words in line 755 help to reinforce the plot?**
4. **According to Galatea, what has Polyphemus' usual behavior been in the past?** (759–761, 768–769) **What does he do now instead?** (764–767) **Why?**
5. **What is Venus' role in this story?** (758–759) **Explain whether or not *alma* (759) is an appropriate description.**
6. **In lines 764–766 Galatea repeats the adverb *iam* four times. This repetition of a word at the beginning of successive clauses is a rhetorical device called *anaphora*. What is the speaker trying to emphasize by this repetition?**
7. **What has the Cyclops lost his thirst for?** (768) **Why is *amor* (768) a good choice of word?**
8. **There are two references in this passage to strangers to the island (*hospite*, 760, and *carīnae*, 769). These probably are meant to make us think of a particular stranger, Odysseus, since he is the only other figure associated with Polyphemus in myth. Such a reference in poetry to a recognizable event or person, real or fictional, outside the poem, is an *allusion*: what is its function here?**

770 ***Tēlemus, -ī** (*m*), the name of a prophet.
Siculus, -a, -um, Sicilian, of Sicily.
***Aetna, -ae** (*f*), Mt. Etna, a volcano in Sicily.
771 **Eurymidēs, -ae** (*m*), the son of Eurymus. **Eurymidēs** is Telemus' patronymic.
āles, ālitis (*m/f*), bird. In Roman religion, soothsayers called augurs observed the flight of birds to discover omens.
772 **Polyphēmon:** Greek accusative singular.
***lūmen, lūminis** (*n*), light, eye.
773 **tibi:** what kind of dative is this?
Ulixēs, Ulixis (*m*), the hero Ulysses (Greek, Odysseus). Homer's epic poem, the *Odyssey*, describes his ten-year voyage home from the Trojan war. Along the way he encounters our Cyclops and blinds him, as Telemus predicts, by driving a stake through his eye as he sleeps, to avenge the death of his shipmates. See "Passages for Comparison."
774 ***rīdeō, rīdēre** (2), **rīsī, rīsum,** to laugh, laugh at.
***vātēs, vātis** (*m*), prophet, seer.
stolidus, -a, -um, stupid, slow.
775 **altera:** to whom does Polyphemus refer? In what two senses is the phrase **lūmen rapere** being used?
776 ***spernō, spernere** (3), **sprēvī, sprētum,** to reject scornfully, spurn.
gradior, gradī (3), **gressus sum**, to step, walk.
***ingēns, ingentis,** huge, vast.
777 **dēgravō** (1), to rest heavily on, press down.
***fessus, -a, -um,** weary, exhausted.
sub: what case does this preposition take here, and why?
***opācus, -a, -um,** shady, dark.
778 ***prōmineō, prōminēre** (2), **prōminuī,** to project, stick out.
***pontus, -ī** (*m*), the sea.
cuneātus, -a, -um, wedge-shaped.
acūmen, acūminis (*n*), peak, promontory.
779 ***aequor, aequoris** (*n*), the sea.
780 **ascendō, ascendere** (3), **ascendī, ascēnsum,** to go up, climb, mount.
resīdō, resīdere (3), **resēdī,** to sit down.
781 ***lāniger, lānigera, lānigerum,** wool-bearing, fleecy.
***pecus, pecudis** (*f*), any farm animal, but especially sheep.
782 **Cui:** dative of agent with **posita est** (783) and **sūmpta . . . est** (784). To what singular noun must this pronoun refer?
***pīnus, -ūs** (*f*), pine (the tree or its wood).
783 ***antemna, -ae** (f), yardarm (the beam that hangs perpendicular to a mast to support a square sail).
***aptus, -a, -um,** useful, appropriate to, suitable for (+ dative).
784 ***harundō, harundinis** (*f*), reed.
conpingō, conpingere (3), **conpēgī, conpāctum,** to attach, bind together.
fistula, -ae (*f*), shepherd's pipe, panpipe (composed of reeds of graduated length bound together in a row).
785 **pastōrius, -a, -um,** of or connected with herdsmen, herdsman's.
sībilum, -ī (*n*), whistling, hissing.
786 **latitō** (1), to lie concealed, be hidden.
rūpis, rūpis (*f*), rocky cliff. **rūpe:** supply **in** or **sub.**
787 **gremium, -ī** (*n*), lap, bosom.
resideō, residēre (2), **resēdī, resessum**, to remain seated, sit.
***auris, auris** (*f*), ear.
788 ***verbum, -ī** (*n*), word.
***notō (1),** to mark, take note of.

II. *A Prophecy Ignored*

Continuing her story, Galatea describes first the Cyclops' response to a soothsayer who warns him about the future and then the way in which love has altered his behavior. In both cases, his actions reveal his character.

"Tēlemus intereā Siculam dēlātus ad Aetnam,
Tēlemus Eurymidēs, quem nūlla fefellerat āles,
terribilem Polyphēmon adit, 'Lūmen,' que, 'quod ūnum
fronte geris mediā, rapiet tibi,' dīxit, 'Ulixēs.'
Rīsit et, 'Ō vātum stolidissime, falleris,' inquit,
'altera iam rapuit.' Sīc frūstrā vēra monentem
spernit et aut gradiēns ingentī lītora passū
dēgravat, aut fessus sub opāca revertitur antra.
Prōminet in pontum cuneātus acūmine longō
collis, utrumque latus circumfluit aequoris unda.
Hūc ferus ascendit Cyclōps mediusque resēdit;
lānigerae pecudēs nūllō dūcente secūtae.
Cui postquam pīnus, baculī quae praebuit ūsum,
ante pedēs posita est antemnīs apta ferendīs
sūmptaque harundinibus conpācta est fistula centum,
sēnsērunt tōtī pastōria sībila montēs,
sēnsērunt undae. Latitāns ego rūpe meīque
Ācidis in gremiō residēns procul auribus hausī
tālia dicta meīs audītaque verba notāvī:

1. **What is Telemus' prophecy?** (772–773) **How does Polyphemus interpret it?** (775) **Will the prophecy come true? In this exchange between Polyphemus and Telemus, Ovid employs a second kind of *irony* (see Baucis and Philemon, 668), whereby one character says something about which either the other character(s) or the audience knows more than he. Explain the irony here and its effect.**
2. **Where and how does Polyphemus now spend his time?** (776–777) **What should he be doing?**
3. **Where is Galatea meanwhile?** (786–787) **What is she doing?** (787–788) **Where does the Cyclops think she is?** (778–780) **(If in doubt, look ahead to 838.) What repeated verb helps bring out the contrast between their activities?**
4. **How large is Polyphemus? What actions or objects reveal his size?** (776, 782–786)
5. **Describe Polyphemus' musical instrument.** (784) **Is there anything unusual about it? How far does his song carry? In poetry an object can represent or *symbolize* an idea or set of ideas: explain how the *fistula* might be a *symbol* of the Cyclops' artistry. What then can we expect of him as a musician?**
6. **Galatea describes the Cyclops as *terribilem* (772) and *ferus* (780). Do these adjectives correctly describe his appearance and actions in this passage? Up to this point in the story, how would you summarize the Cyclops' character?**

789 **Candidior foliō:** this construction is repeated over and over until line 807. Explain it.
***niveus, -a, -um,** snowy. **ligustrum, -ī** (*n*), a white-flowered shrub, such as privet.
790 **flōridus, -a, -um,** flowery, blooming. **prātum, -ī** (*n*), meadow.
***prōcērus, -a, -um,** tall, lofty. **alnus, -ī** (*f*), an alder tree.
791 **splendidus, -a, -um,** bright, shining. **vitrum, -ī** (*n*), glass.
***lascīvus, -a, -um,** playful, frisky, frolicsome. ***haedus, -ī** (*m*), young goat, kid.
792 **lēvis, -is, -e,** smooth. **adsiduus, -a, -um,** unceasing, restless.
dēterō, dēterere (3), **dētrīvī, dētrītum,** to wear down, wear away.
concha, -ae (*f*), seashell.
793 **hībernus, -a, -um,** wintry. **sōlibus hībernīs:** what comparative adjective must you supply?
aestīvus, -a, -um, summery, of summer. ***umbra, -ae** (*f*), shade.
794 ***pōmum, -ī** (*n*), fruit tree, fruit. **platanus, -ī** (*f*), plane tree.
cōnspectus, -a, -um, visible, conspicuous.
795 **lūcidus, -a, -um,** bright, clear, translucent.
glaciēs, -ēī (*f*), ice. **dulcis, -is, -e,** sweet.
796 **cygnus (cycnus) -ī** (*m*), swan.
***plūma, -ae** (*f*), feather.
797 **fugiās:** how do you explain the subjunctive?
***fōrmōsus, -a, -um,** beautiful, fair.
798 ***saevus, -a, -um,** savage, ferocious. **indomitus, -a, -um,** untamed, wild.
***iuvenca, -ae** (*f*), young cow, heifer; or **iuvencus, -ī** (*m*), young bull, bullock.
799 **annōsus, -a, -um,** full of years, aged.
***fallāx, fallācis,** deceitful, deceptive.
800 **lentus, -a, -um,** tough, pliant. **salix, salicis** (*f*), willow tree.
virga, -ae (*f*), rod, twig.
***albus, -a, -um,** white. **vītis alba,** white bryony, a climbing European vine.
801 ***scopulus, -ī** (*m*), rock, boulder. ***amnis, amnis** (*m/f*), river, current.
802 **pāvō, pāvōnis** (*m*), peacock. **superbus, -a, -um,** proud, haughty.
803 **asper, aspera, asperum,** harsh, prickly.
tribulus, -ī (*m*), a spiny plant, bramble.
fētus, -a, -um, pregnant, having recently given birth.
truculentus, -a, -um, ferocious, aggressive. ***ursa, -ae** (*f*), she-bear.
804 **surdus, -a, -um,** deaf, unresponsive.
calcō (1), to trample, tread on. **hydrus, -ī** (*m*), watersnake, snake.
805 **quod . . . possem:** the antecedent is expressed in the following lines (806–807). **vellem** is subjunctive in a contrary-to-fact conditional sentence. Supply a protasis such as "If it were possible. . . ." **Volō** may take the subjunctive in an optative construction.
praecipuē, especially.
***dēmō, dēmere** (3), **dēmpsī, dēmptum,** to remove, take away.
806 **nōn tantum . . . vērum etiam** (807): not only . . . but also.
***cervus, -ī** (*m*), stag. **cervō . . . āctō:** look for the comparative adjective in 807.
***clārus, -a, -um,** loud, clear.
lātrātus, -ūs (*m*), barking, baying (of dogs).
807 ***volucer, volucris, volucre,** flying, swift.
***fugāx, fugācis,** fleeting, swift. ***aura, -ae** (*f*), air, breeze.
808 **nōris:** = **nōveris**, perfect subjunctive in a future less vivid condition. **at bene sī nōris:** supply **mē.**
piget, pigēre (2), **piguit** (*impersonal*), it irks, displeases. **pigeat**: supply **tē** as both object of **pigeat** and subject of the infinitive **fūgisse**.
809 ***damnō** (1), to condemn, reject.

III. *Song of the Cyclops*

At first Polyphemus can only praise Galatea, but then he remembers things about her he does not like. Because he compares her to many things around him, his song also tells us about the world in which he lives.

" 'Candidior foliō niveī, Galatēa, ligustrī,
flōridior prātīs, longā prōcērior alnō,
splendidior vitrō, tenerō lascīvior haedō,
lēvior adsiduō dētrītīs aequore conchīs,
sōlibus hībernīs, aestīvā grātior umbrā,
nōbilior pōmīs, platanō cōnspectior altā,
lūcidior glaciē, mātūrā dulcior ūvā,
mollior et cygnī plūmīs et lacte coāctō,
et, sī nōn fugiās, riguō fōrmōsior hortō:
saevior indomitīs eadem Galatēa iuvencīs,
dūrior annōsā quercū, fallācior undīs,
lentior et salicis virgīs et vītibus albīs,
hīs inmōbilior scopulīs, violentior amne,
laudātō pāvōne superbior, ācrior ignī,
asperior tribulīs, fētā truculentior ursā,
surdior aequoribus, calcātō inmītior hydrō,
et, quod praecipuē vellem tibi dēmere possem,
nōn tantum cervō clārīs lātrātibus āctō,
vērum etiam ventīs volucrīque fugācior aurā
(at bene sī nōris, pigeat fūgisse, morāsque
ipsa tuās damnēs et mē retinēre labōrēs).

1. **How many comparisons does Polyphemus make? Why does he make so many? What thought makes him change his tune in the middle?** (797)
2. **What does Polyphemus say Galatea would do if she knew him better?** (808–809) **Explain whether these actions are likely.**
3. **List the qualities of Galatea that Polyphemus admires, then the qualities he dislikes. In general what does he like about her? What does he dislike? What is the result of his expressing his emotions like this, rather than naming her qualities directly?**
4. **Remember that Galatea is a sea nymph. Which of these compliments do you think she would find pleasing? How many of the criticisms would she understand and resent?**
5. **The Cyclops' praise of Galatea, because it is formed of comparisons, reveals to us the elements that make up the giant's world. Briefly summarize this world. How might it differ from the world of the poet's audience?**
6. **What new information about Polyphemus' character does this song give us?**

810 **Sunt mihi:** what kind of dative is this? This construction is repeated with **sunt** in 812, 813, and 814.
pendeō, pendēre (2), **pependī,** to hang, be supported over a vault. **pendentia:** "vaulted."
811 **quibus:** supply **in.**
812 **gravō** (1), to weigh down, load.
813 ***aurum, -ī** (*n*), gold.
815 **Ipsa** (repeated in 816): the adjective intensifies the subject of **legēs.** See 825 for the same usage.
silvestris, silvestris, silvestre, wooded, woodland.
816 **frāga, -ōrum** (*n pl*), wild strawberries.
legō, legere (3), **lēgī, lēctum,** to gather, pick.
817 **līveō, līvēre** (2), to be livid, dull blue, discolored.
***sūcus, -ī** (*m*), the juice of a plant or fruit.
818 **generōsus, -a, -um,** noble, choice, superior.
imitor, imitārī (1), **imitātus sum,** to imitate, resemble.
819 **castanea, -ae** (*f*), chestnut (tree or fruit).
mē coniuge: ablative absolute. **dēerunt**: pronounced as two syllables.
820 **arbuteus, -a, -um,** of the arbutus or wild strawberry tree.
fētus, -ūs (*m*), offspring, fruit.
821 **multae:** supply **pecudēs** (*f pl*) as the subject. Ovid uses the collective neuter noun **(pecus, pecoris)** in the first part of the line but implies the feminine **pecus, pecudis** in the second half.
***errō** (1), to wander, roam.
822 **stabulō** (1), to house (domestic animals).
823 Explain the use of the three subjunctives: **rogēs, possim,** and **sint.**
***quot**, how many?
824 **pauperis** is a predicate genitive modifying the subject infinitive **numerāre.** An idiomatic translation for this use of the predicate genitive is, "It is the mark of a poor man to. . . ."
numerō (1), to add up, count.
825 ***nīl:** = **nihil.**
crēdideris: perfect subjunctive in a future less vivid condition; supply in translation an introductory clause such as, "If I were to tell you. . . ."
826 **circumeant:** "surround." The subject is still **pecudēs** (from **hārum,** 824). Why is the verb subjunctive?
distendō, distendere (3), **distendī, distentum,** to swell, distend, fill to bursting.
crūs, crūris (*n*), leg. **crūribus:** ablative of means. The Cyclops exaggerates how full the cows' udders are.
ūber, ūberis (*n*), udder.
827 **fētūra, -ae** (*f*), young offspring. **fētūra minor:** in apposition to **agnī.**
***ovīle, ovīlis** (*n*), pen for sheep, sheepfold.
agnus, -ī (*m*), lamb.
828 **pār aetās:** translate as if **parēs aetāte.**
829 ***bibō, bibere** (3), **bibī,** to drink.
830 ***liquefaciō, liquefacere** (3), **liquefēcī, liquefactum,** to melt, dissolve.
coāgulum, -ī (*n*), rennet, the inner lining of the fourth stomach of calves (a dried extract of this lining added to milk curdles it so as to produce cheese).
***dūrō** (1), to harden, solidify.

IV. *Promises, Promises*

Polyphemus, in cataloguing the gifts he would like to give Galatea, reveals his own values. Will these presents please Galatea?

" 'Sunt mihi, pars montis, vīvō pendentia saxō
antra, quibus nec sōl mediō sentītur in aestū
nec sentītur hiems; sunt pōma gravantia rāmōs;
sunt aurō similēs longīs in vītibus ūvae,
sunt et purpureae: tibi et hās servāmus et illās.
Ipsa tuīs manibus silvestrī nāta sub umbrā
mollia frāga legēs, ipsa autumnalia corna
prūnaque, nōn sōlum nigrō līventia sūcō,
vērum etiam generōsa novāsque imitantia cērās;
nec tibi castaneae mē coniuge, nec tibi deerunt
arbuteī fētūs: omnis tibi serviet arbor.
Hoc pecus omne meum est; multae quoque vallibus errant,
multās silva tegit, multae stabulantur in antrīs,
nec, sī forte rogēs, possim tibi dīcere, quot sint.
Pauperis est numerāre pecus! Dē laudibus hārum
nīl mihi crēdideris: praesēns potes ipsa vidēre,
ut vix circumeant distentum crūribus ūber.
Sunt, fētūra minor, tepidīs in ovīlibus agnī,
sunt quoque, pār aetās, aliīs in ovīlibus haedī.
Lac mihi semper adest niveum: pars inde bibenda
servātur, partem liquefacta coāgula dūrant.

1. **What important condition underlies all the Cyclops' offers?** (819)
2. **Occasionally Polyphemus imagines Galatea as his companion (815–818, 825–826). What does he think she will be doing?**
3. **Draw up a list of Polyphemus' gifts. What kinds of things will he give Galatea? How has he organized his list of gifts? How does he describe them? In what ways is Polyphemus' song different from the simple list you have made?**
4. **What characteristics about himself does this song of the Cyclops reveal?** (820–826)
5. **To what qualities in Galatea does the Cyclops hope to appeal with these offers?**
6. **How many instances of anaphora are there in this passage? What in each case is the effect of the repetition?**
7. **Galatea has described Polyphemus as a savage barbarian, combing his hair with rakes and having to practice civilized facial expressions in a mirror (765–767). Explain whether or not this is the kind of song you would expect a savage to sing.**

831 **dēliciae, -ārum** (*f pl*), luxuries, toys.
vulgō (1), to make available to the mass of the population, to make common.
832 ***contingō, contingere** (3), **contigī, contāctum** (+ *dat.*), to fall to one's lot.
damma, -ae (*f*), general name for various members of the deer family, such as red deer and gazelle.
lepus, leporis (*m*), hare.
caper, caprī (*m*), billygoat, he-goat.
833 **pār, paris** (*n*), a pair.
columba, -ae (*f*) dove, pigeon.
nīdus, -ī (*m*), nest.
834 **geminōs:** modifying **catulōs** (836).
***lūdō, lūdere (3), lūsī, lūsum,** to play, have fun.
possint: what kind of subjunctive is this?
835 **dīnōscō, dīnōscere** (3), to distinguish, tell apart.
836 **villōsus, -a, -um,** shaggy, hairy.
catulus, -ī (*m*), the young of any land mammal, cub, etc.
837 **domina, -ae** (*f*), female head of household, mistress, powerful beloved.
servābimus: like Galatea (752, 757), Polyphemus uses the poetic first-person plural. See also 839.
838 ***caeruleus (caerulus), -a, -um,** blue, blue-green.
***nitidus, -a, -um,** bright, radiant, gleaming.
exerō, exerere (3), **exeruī, exertum,** to stretch forth, put forth.
840 ***imāgō, imāginis** (*f*), reflection, image.
841 **nūper,** recently, lately.
842 ***adspiciō, adspicere** (3), **adspexī, adspectum,** to observe, look at, gaze upon.
hōc corpore: why is this phrase ablative?
843 ***soleō, solēre** (2), **solitus sum** (+ *infinitive*), to be accustomed.
844 **nescio quem . . . Iovem:** "some Jupiter or other" (with the idea of unimportance).
coma, -ae (*f*), hair.
plūrimus, -a, um, very much, the greatest amount of.
torvus, -a, -um, grim, fierce.
845 **umerus, -ī** (*m*), shoulder.
lūcus, -ī (*m*), grove, woods.
obumbrō (1), to darken, overshadow, shade.
846 **mea . . . corpora** (847): poetic plural, used instead of the singular to mean the entire body. See also 848.
***rigidus, -a, -um,** rigid, stiff.
dēnsissima: translate as an adverb modifying **horrent.**
***saeta, -ae** (*f*), coarse or stiff animal hair.
847 ***frōns, frondis** (*f*), foliage.
848 ***collum, -ī** (*n*), neck. **colla . . . flāventia:** poetic plural.
iuba, -ae (*f*), mane.
849 **ovis, ovis** (*f*), sheep.
lāna, -ae (*f*), wool.
***decus, decōris** (*n*), distinction, glory. **ovibus . . . decōrī:** datives of reference and purpose (double dative).
850 **hirtus, -a, -um,** hairy, shaggy, rough.
***decet, decēre** (2), **decuit,** (*impersonal*) it is becoming, fitting, (*personal*) add grace to, adorn.
851 **īnstar** (*n, indeclinable*) (+ *gen.*), the equal.
852 **clipeus, -ī** (*m*), round shield.
853 **orbis, orbis** (*m*), disk, sphere.

V. *The Greatest Gift of All*

Finally, Polyphemus offers himself, describing in detail several of his more important features. This self-portrait reveals not only his physical qualities, but some inner characteristics as well.

" 'Nec tibi dēliciae facilēs vulgātaque tantum
mūnera contingent, dammae leporēsque caperque,
pārque columbārum dēmptusque cacūmine nīdus:
invēnī geminōs, quī tēcum lūdere possint,
inter sē similēs, vix ut dīnōscere possīs,
villōsae catulōs in summīs montibus ursae;
invēnī et dīxī, 'Dominae servābimus istōs.'
Iam modo caeruleō nitidum caput exere pontō,
iam, Galatēa, venī nec mūnera dēspice nostra!
Certē ego mē nōvī liquidaeque in imāgine vīdī
nūper aquae, placuitque mihi mea forma videntī.
Adspice, sim quantus: nōn est hōc corpore maior
Iuppiter in caelō (nam vōs nārrāre solētis
nescio quem rēgnāre Iovem), coma plūrima torvōs
prōminet in vultūs umerōsque, ut lūcus, obumbrat,
nec, mea quod rigidīs horrent dēnsissima saetīs
corpora, turpe putā: turpis sine frondibus arbor,
turpis equus, nisi colla iubae flāventia vēlent;
plūma tegit volucrēs, ovibus sua lāna decōrī est:
barba virōs hirtaeque decent in corpore saetae.
Ūnum est in mediā lūmen mihi fronte, sed īnstar
ingentis clipeī. Quid? Nōn haec omnia magnus
Sōl videt ē caelō? Sōlī tamen ūnicus orbis.

1. **What is the Cyclops' attitude toward gifts such as deer or doves?** (831–833) **What other gifts will he offer Galatea?** (834–837) **What qualities make his gifts special?**
2. **What does Polyphemus want Galatea to do?** (838–839) **What is she doing instead?** (786–788) **How does this ironic situation affect our view of Polyphemus and Galatea?**
3. **Where has Polyphemus seen himself?** (840–841) **How does his view of himself compare with Galatea's view of him?** (765–767)
4. **How does Polyphemus explain away his physical defects: *coma* (844), *saetīs* (846), and *ūnum . . . lūmen* (851)?**
5. **What does this description of the Cyclops reveal about his character?**
6. **What is the *simile* in 851–852? (A simile is an explicit comparison of one thing with another, signaled by the presence of "like" or "as.") How is it a clue to Polyphemus' size?**
7. **What is the Cyclops' attitude toward Jupiter?** (842–844) **Remember also that Galatea has earlier said that Polyphemus is *magnī cum dīs contemptor Olympī* (761). Explain whether or not, in the ancient world, this is a good attitude to have. What is likely to be the result of it? What event do we know lies in Polyphemus' future?**

854 ***addō, addere** (3), **addidī, additum,** to consider additionally, take into account as well.
genitor, genitōris (*m*), one's father. **genitor meus:** i.e., Neptune, ruling god of the sea.
855 **socer, socerī** (*m*), father-in-law.
misereor, miserērī (2), **miseritus sum** (+ *gen.*), to pity. **miserēre:** imperative.
856 **supplex, supplicis,** making humble entreaty, suppliant.
exaudiō (4), to pay heed to, understand.
succumbō, succumbere (3), **succubuī, succubitum,** to submit to, yield to. This verb is usually used to describe a woman yielding to a man. How does that usage affect the meaning here?
857 **quīque . . . spernō:** = **et ego, quī spernō.**
penetrābilis, -is, -e, capable of penetrating, piercing.
***fulmen, fulminis** (*n*), lightning, thunderbolt.
858 **Nērēis, Nērēidis** (*f*), daughter of Nereus. Polyphemus calls upon Galatea by her patronymic. **Nērei:** vocative.
veneror, venerārī (1), **venerātus sum,** to worship, adore. ***īra, -ae** (*f*), anger, rage.
859 **contemptus, -ūs** (*m*), contempt, scorn.
patiēns, patientis (+ *gen.*), able or willing to endure or undergo.
essem . . . fugerēs (860): explain these two subjunctives.
860 ***repellō, repellere** (3), **reppulī, repulsum,** to push or drive away, repel, rebuff.
861 **Ācin:** accusative.
praeferō, praeferre (*irreg.*), **praetulī, praelātum,** to esteem more highly, prefer to (+ dative).
***conplexus, -ūs** (*m*), embrace, grasp.
862 **placeat . . . sibī placeat . . . tibī** (863): both verbs depend upon **licēbit,** which takes the subjunctive with the meaning "although."
863 **quod nōllem:** the apodosis of a contrary-to-fact condition, understood; supply a clause (protasis) such as, "If I had my way. . . ." The relative pronoun refers to the entire idea contained in line 861.
modo cōpia dētur: supply **mihi. modo . . . dētur:** clause of proviso with subjunctive. **cōpia:** "opportunity."
864 **mihī:** what kind of dative is this? **prō**: "in proportion to," "in conformity with."
865 **viscus, visceris** (*n*), internal organs of the body.
866 ***spargō, spargere** (3), **sparsī, sparsum,** to scatter, sprinkle.
tibi: "with you," dative of reference. Erotic meaning with **sē misceat.**
867 **laedō, laedere** (3), **laesī, laesum,** to injure, pain, wrong in love.
exaestuō (1), to boil, seethe, rage. **ignis:** supply **meus.**
868 **suīs . . . vīribus:** i.e., of Mt. Etna. What special forces does this mountain have?
trānsferō, trānsferre (*irreg.*), **trānstulī, trānslātum,** to convey, transport.
869 ***pectus, pectoris** (*n*), breast.
870 **nēquīquam,** in vain. ***queror, querī** (3), **questus sum,** to complain, protest.
***cūnctus, -a, -um,** the whole of, all.
871 ***surgō, surgere** (3), **surrēxī, surrēctum,** to rise to one's feet, get up.
taurus, -ī (*m*), bull. **ut taurus:** how does Galatea's simile affect our sense of the Cyclops' character? Does it make him more sympathetic? laughable? fearful?
vacca, -ae (*f*), cow. **furibundus, -a, -um,** maddened, frenzied.
***adimō, adimere** (3), **adēmī, adēmptum,** to take away, deprive of.
872 **nequeō, nequīre** (*irreg.*), **nequīvī (nequiī),** to be unable to (+ infinitive).
silvā: supply **in. saltus, -ūs** (*m*), woodland, glade.
873 **ignārus, -a, -um,** ignorant, unaware. **ignārōs nec . . . timentēs**: accusative plurals modifying **mē . . . atque Ācin** (874).
874 **exclāmō** (1), to cry out. **ista ultima** (875) **sit:** supply **ut**. What kind of clause is this?
875 **Veneris . . . vestrae:** by metonymy, the goddess of love stands for the love between Acis and Galatea.
concordia, -ae (*f*), friendship, harmony, union.

VI. *The Betrayal*

Polyphemus concludes his appeal with one last, irresistible offer. Puzzled by Galatea's preferences, he finally realizes his situation, promising a violent, but—as he sees it—fitting end to his rival.

" 'Adde, quod in vestrō genitor meus aequore rēgnat:
hunc tibi dō socerum. Tantum miserēre precēsque
supplicis exaudī! Tibi enim succumbimus ūnī,
quīque Iovem et caelum spernō et penetrābile fulmen,
Nērei, tē veneror: tua fulmine saevior īra est.
Atque ego contemptūs essem patientior huius,
sī fugerēs omnēs; sed cūr Cyclōpe repulsō
Ācin amās, praefersque meīs conplexibus Ācin?
Ille tamen placeatque sibī placeatque licēbit,
quod nōllem, Galatēa, tibī: modo cōpia dētur,
sentiet esse mihī tantō prō corpore vīrēs.
Viscera vīva traham dīvīsaque membra per agrōs,
perque tuās spargam (sīc sē tibi misceat!) undās.
Ūror enim, laesusque exaestuat ācrius ignis,
cumque suīs videor trānslātam vīribus Aetnam
pectore ferre meō: nec tū, Galatēa, movēris!'
Tālia nēquīquam questus (nam cūncta vidēbam)
surgit et ut taurus vaccā furibundus adēmptā
stāre nequit silvāque et nōtīs saltibus errat:
cum ferus ignārōs nec quicquam tāle timentēs
mē videt atque Ācin, 'Videō,' que exclāmat, 'et ista
ultima sit, faciam, Veneris concordia vestrae.'

1. **Whom does Polyphemus promise to give Galatea for a father-in-law?** (854–855) **Why should Galatea be tempted by this promise?**
2. **What is the Cyclops' attitude toward Galatea in this passage? How does he compare her to Jupiter?** (855–858)
3. **What makes Galatea's rejection of Polyphemus unbearable to him?** (859–860)
4. **What question does Polyphemus ask Galatea?** (860–861) **What is the answer likely to be? What does the fact that he has to ask it reveal about his character and his situation?**
5. **What death does Polyphemus threaten to give Acis?** (865–866) **Why does he think it a suitable one?**
6. **A *metaphor* is like a simile in that it makes a comparison, but the comparison is implied, not stated, and thus omits "like" or "as." In lines 868–869 identify Polyphemus' metaphor. What two things are being compared? What is the effect of the comparison?**
7. **When the Cyclops sees Acis and Galatea, what does he promise?** (874–875) **Given the Cyclops' character and capabilities, what is likely to happen?**

876 ***īrātus, -a, -um,** angry, enraged.
877 ***clāmor, clāmōris** (*m*), shout, shouting, roar.
perhorrēscō, perhorrēscere (3), **perhorruī,** to tremble greatly, be greatly frightened of.
878 **ast,** but, thereupon. ***vīcīnus, -a, -um,** neighboring.
pavefaciō, pavefacere (3), **pavefēcī, pavefactum,** to terrify, alarm.
879 **convertō, convertere** (3), **convertī, conversum,** to turn about. **terga . . . conversa:** "he turned his back in flight."
Symaethius, -a, -um, of the river Symaethus or its god. Symaethus was Acis' grandfather (see line 750).
hērōs, herōos (*m*) (*Greek loan word*), hero.
880 ***precor, precārī** (1), **precātus sum,** to ask or pray for something.
882 **īnsequor, īnsequī** (3), **īnsecūtus sum,** to follow in the track of, pursue.
Īnsequitur . . . Ācin (882-884): how do these lines help us visualize the relative sizes of the two characters?
revellō, revellere (3), **revellī, revulsum,** to tear loose, wrench off.
883 ***quamvīs,** although. ***perveniō, pervenīre** (4), **pervēnī, perventum,** to get to, reach, land on.
884 **angulus, -ī** (*m*), angle, corner, projecting point. **tōtum:** translate as if an adverb.
obruō, obruere (3), **obruī, obrutum,** to crush, overwhelm, bury.
885 **nōs . . . fēcimus** (886): as a nymph, Galatea has some supernatural powers. She is the agent of the following metamorphosis.
886 ***adsūmō, adsūmere** (3), **adsūmpsī, adsūmptum,** to take possession of, acquire.
ut . . . adsūmeret: what kind of clause is this?
avītus, -a, -um, of or belonging to a grandfather. **vīrēs . . . avītās:** what kind of powers might Acis' grandfather have had?
887 **pūniceus, -a, -um,** scarlet, crimson. The ancient Carthaginians (Latin, **Pūnicī**) manufactured a precious purple dye from the murex, a salt-water mollusk. Because of their monopoly over this process, their name came to be synonymous with the color of the dye.
***mōlēs, mōlis** (*f*), a large mass, boulder.
mānō (1), to flow, run, drip.
888 ***rubor, rubōris** (*m*), redness.
ēvānēscō, ēvānēscere (3), **ēvānuī,** to vanish, fade away.
889 ***turbō (1),** to agitate, disturb, muddy.
imber, imbris (*m*), rain. Read the line as **color flūminis turbātī prīmō imbre.**
890 **purgō** (1), to free from impurities, cleanse, purify.
tacta: i.e., by Galatea.
dehiscō, dehiscere (3), to split open, yawn, gape.
891 **rīma, -ae** (*f*), crack, fissure.
892 **ōs . . . undīs**: a fountain pours out of the opening that Galatea's touch has created.
***sonō, sonāre** (1), **sonuī, sonitum,** to make a noise, sound.
exsultō (1), to spring up, dance.
893 **tenus** (+ *abl.*), right up to, as far as.
exstō, exstāre (1), **exstitī,** to stand out, be conspicuous.
alvus, -ī (*m*), belly, stomach.
894 **incinctus, -a, -um,** wrapped tightly around, girt.
***iuvenis, iuvenis** (*m*), young man.
nova cornua: accusative of specification. **incinctus . . . flexīs nova cornua cannīs:** "girt round his new horns with pliant reeds."
895 **nisi quod:** "except that." Supply **erat.**
caerulus: = **caeruleus** (see 838).
896 **Ācis erat:** the story ends the way it began (see line 750).
897 **antīquus, -a, -um,** former.
898 **dēsinō, dēsinere** (3), **dēs(i)ī (dēsīvī), dēsitum,** to leave off, desist.

VII. *The Death of Acis*

As Galatea finishes her story, she explains how she escaped Polyphemus' attack but how Acis did not. Nevertheless, the young man's plea for help did not go unheeded, as his metamorphosis shows.

"Tantaque vōx, quantam Cyclōps īrātus habēre
dēbuit, illa fuit: clāmōre perhorruit Aetna.
Ast ego vīcīnō pavefacta sub aequore mergor;
terga fugae dederat conversa Symaethius hērōs
et, 'Fer opem, Galatēa, precor, mihi! ferte, parentēs,'
dīxerat, 'et vestrīs peritūrum admittite rēgnīs.'
Īnsequitur Cyclōps partemque ē monte revulsam
mittit, et, extrēmus quamvīs pervēnit ad illum
angulus ē saxō, tōtum tamen obruit Ācin;
at nōs, quod sōlum fierī per fāta licēbat,
fēcimus, ut vīrēs adsūmeret Ācis avītās.
Pūniceus dē mōle cruor mānābat, et intrā
temporis exiguum rubor ēvānēscere coepit,
fitque color prīmō turbātī flūminis imbre
purgāturque morā; tum mōlēs tacta dehiscit,
vīvaque per rīmās prōcēraque surgit harundō,
ōsque cavum saxī sonat exsultantibus undīs:
mīraque rēs, subitō mediā tenus exstitit alvō
incinctus iuvenis flexīs nova cornua cannīs,
quī, nisi quod maior, quod tōtō caerulus ōre,
Ācis erat. Et sīc quoque erat tamen Ācis in amnem
versus, et antīquum tenuērunt flūmina nōmen."
Dēsierat Galatēa loquī.

1. **What does Galatea do when she hears Polyphemus shout?** (878)
2. **To whom does Acis pray, and for what?** (880–881) **Are his actions appropriate for a hero, or is *hērōs* an ironic designation?**
3. **How does Polyphemus kill Acis?** (882–884)
4. ***Cyclops . . . mittit* (882–883): with this action, we see the last of Polyphemus. Taken all in all, what is his character? Is his action surprising, or in keeping? Is his action justified, or is he a villain?**
5. **Although Galatea cannot rescue Acis, what can she do for him?** (885–886)
6. **What happens to the rock that buried Acis?** (887–892)
7. **How has Acis' physical appearance changed? What is he wearing?** (893–896)
8. **The poem says, *Ācis erat* (896). Was it Acis or not? How much can one change and still be the same person?**
9. **In the introduction to this story Ovid portrays Galatea weeping as she tells her story. Is the story sad? If so, for whom are we to feel sorrow?**

NARCISSUS AND ECHO

Narcissus and His Reflection, mosaic from Antioch

344 **ēnītor, ēnītī** (3), **ēnīxus sum,** to give birth.
uterus, -ī (*m*), womb.
345 **nymphē**: Greek spelling of nominative gives ending in **-ē** rather than the Latin lst declension **-a**. Narcissus' mother was named Liriope. Narcissus, lovable at birth, will perish at 16, so lovable that he will have loved himself fatally.
346 **esset**: with **vīsūrus** (347), "whether he would see."
348 **fātidicus, -a, -um**, speaking fate, prophetic.
vātēs: i.e, Teresias, the blind prophet, who plays a major role in many Theban myths. He infallibly predicts the future. Here, Narcissus is doomed by self-knowledge that would seem to most people a very desirable asset. Watch how Ovid works out this prediction.
349 **augur, auguris** (*m*), a prophet who interprets bird signs.
350 **furor, furōris** (*m*), madness. Narcissus' self-knowledge will be a fatal kind of "insanity."
351 **quīnī, -ae, -a**, five each. Ovid plays games with us: add 1 year to 3 x 5 and you get 16 years old.
Cēphīsius: i.e., Narcissus, son of the river-god Cephisus.
352 **puer**: Narcissus at 16 is still a boy and not quite a young man.
354 **superbia, -ae** (*f*), pride.
355 **nūllī** . . . **iuvenēs, nūllae** . . . **puellae**: note the parallel arrangement of words.

356 **agitō** (1), to drive.
rētium, -ī (*n*), net. A regular pastime of men in Greek myth is hunting.
357 **vōcālis, -is, -e**, possessing a voice, speaking. This nymph is Echo, who, though not yet reduced to voice alone, is defined even now by her voice. See lines 359 and 399.
***reticēre**: "to give no reply to" (+ dative).
358 **resonābilis, -is, -e**, responding, echoing. Ovid coined this word here. Echo's current habits will soon become the limits of her physical abilities.
360 **garrulus, -a, -um**, talkative.
361 **verba novissima**: "the last words" (because most recent).
posset: explain the subjunctive.
362 **dēprendō, dēprendere** (3), **dēprēnsī, dēprēnsum** (*shortened or syncopated form of* **dēprehendō**), to catch, seize. Jealous Juno is always catching or trying to catch the women whom her lusty, unfaithful husband Jupiter chases.
364 **prūdēns**: Echo deliberately delayed Juno by her chatter in order to help her sister-nymphs escape.
365 **fugerent**: subjunctive with **dum** indicating purpose, "until they should flee."

OVID, *METAMORPHOSES* III.344–510

I. *The Young Hunter and His Admirers*

A nymph gives birth to Narcissus. His lovable appearance is countered by two problems: a paradoxical prophecy of short life and his haughty treatment of others, which renders him unlovable because unloving.

Ēnīxa est uterō pulcherrima plēnō
īnfantem nymphē, iam tunc quī posset amārī,
Narcissumque vocat; dē quō cōnsultus, an esset
tempora mātūrae vīsūrus longa senectae,
fātidicus vātēs, "Sī sē nōn nōverit," inquit.
Vāna diū vīsa est vōx auguris, exitus illam
rēsque probat lētīque genus novitāsque furōris.
Namque ter ad quīnōs ūnum Cēphīsius annum
addiderat poteratque puer iuvenisque vidērī:
multī illum iuvenēs, multae cupiēre puellae;
sed (fuit in tenerā tam dūra superbia fōrmā)
nūllī illum iuvenēs, nūllae tetigēre puellae.

The nymph Echo admires Narcissus as he goes hunting. Echo has been punished by Juno and has lost the power of independent speech. She can only try to use the final words of others to express her feelings.

Adspicit hunc trepidōs agitantem in rētia cervōs
vōcālis nymphē, quae nec reticēre loquentī
nec prius ipsa loquī didicit, resonābilis Ēchō.
Corpus adhūc Ēchō, nōn vōx erat; et tamen ūsum
garrula nōn alium, quam nunc habet, ōris habēbat,
reddere dē multīs ut verba novissima posset.
Fēcerat hoc Iūnō, quia, cum dēprendere posset
sub Iove saepe suō nymphās in monte iacentēs,
illa deam longō prūdēns sermōne tenēbat,
dum fugerent nymphae.

1. **What was remarkable about Narcissus even as a newborn baby?** (345)
2. **What was the prophet asked about the child? What was his answer? What did it mean?** (346–348)
3. **Did the prophecy prove true? If so, when?** (349–350)
4. **Was Narcissus popular as a young man? What was the reason? How did he respond to those who sought his friendship and love?** (353–355)
5. **What was Narcissus doing when Echo first saw him?** (356)
6. **Describe the peculiar nature of Echo. How does her nature differ from the usual conception of an echo?** (357–361)
7. **How had Echo provoked the vengeance of Juno?** (362–365)
8. **What features in Echo make her into a dependent type?**
9. **If Narcissus has ignored women who are not disabled, what might we expect about Echo's chances of attracting and winning him?**

365 **Sāturnia, -ae** (*f*), Juno, daughter of Saturn.
366 **dēlūdō, dēlūdere** (3), **dēlūsī, dēlūsum**, to fool, deceive.
368 **firmō** (1), to confirm. **Rē . . . minās firmat**: Juno punishes Echo by restricting her speech to repetition of a few final syllables spoken by another.
369 **ingeminō** (1), to double, repeat.

370 **dēvius, -a, -um**, remote, out-of-the-way.
rūs, rūris (*n*), the country. Narcissus is hunting.
371 **incalēscō, incalēscere** (3), **incaluī**, to grow warm, get excited, become impassioned. This is an emphatic compound of **calēscō**, which appears in line 372. The fire metaphor continues through line 374.
fūrtim, secretly.
372 **quōque magis**: "and by how much more," "and the more."
propior, propius, nearer.
flammā propiōre: ablative of cause.
373 **nōn aliter quam**: lit., "not otherwise than" = "just as," a common Ovidian way of starting a simile.
circumlinō, circumlinere (3), ———, **circumlitum**, to smear all over. The participle here takes the dative **taedīs** and modifies **sulphura** (374).
taeda, -ae (*f*), torch.
374 **admōtās**: with **flammās**.
375 **blandus, -a, -um**, flattering, charming.
dictum, -ī (*n*), word. **dictīs**, ablative of manner.
376 **repugnō** (1), to oppose, prevent. Ovid stresses Echo's frustration; her physical limitations block her from doing what she wants.
377 **sinit**: supply **ut** with **incipiat**.
quod sinit: "what [Nature] does allow." This parenthetical remark Ovid now proceeds to explain.
378 ***sonus, -ī** (*m*), sound.
remittat: subjunctive in a relative clause of characteristic.
379 **puer . . . sēductus**: Narcissus, last mentioned in line 370, now appears to be most conveniently alone and accessible to Echo.
sēdūcō, sēdūcere (3), **sēdūxī, sēductum**, to draw away, separate.
380 **adest**: here Ovid artfully starts his echo effects; in Narcissus' last word or words, Echo has an answer.
381 **aciēs, aciēī** (*f*), line of battle, sharp glance.
pars, partis (*f*), part, direction.
dīmittō, dīmittere (3), **dīmīsī, dīmissum**, to cast about.
382 **vocantem**: supply **eum**. Echo also says "**Venī**."
383 **respiciō, respicere** (3), **respexī, respectum**, to look back.
nūllō veniente: ablative absolute.
quid, why.
384 **quot**: Echo uses the same words.

II. *Futile Echo*

Juno had punished Echo by causing the first stage of the change that would finally turn the nymph into the bodiless echo that we know.

Postquam hoc Sāturnia sēnsit,
"Huius," ait, "linguae, quā sum dēlūsa, potestās
parva tibi dabitur vōcisque brevissimus ūsus."
Rēque minās firmat; tamen haec in fīne loquendī
ingeminat vōcēs audītaque verba reportat.

Passionately waiting for Narcissus to speak, Echo at last gets her chance. While the two are at a distance and Narcissus cannot see his admirer, a conversation develops. It is desperate for Echo and utterly puzzling for Narcissus.

Ergō ubi Narcissum per dēvia rūra vagantem
vīdit et incaluit, sequitur vēstīgia fūrtim,
quōque magis sequitur, flammā propiōre calēscit,
nōn aliter quam cum summīs circumlita taedīs
admōtās rapiunt vīvācia sulphura flammās.
Ō quotiēns voluit blandīs accēdere dictīs
et mollēs adhibēre precēs! Nātūra repugnat
nec sinit incipiat; sed, quod sinit, illa parāta est
exspectāre sonōs, ad quōs sua verba remittat.
Forte puer comitum sēductus ab agmine fīdō
dīxerat, "Ecquis adest?" et, "Adest," responderat Ēchō.
Hic stupet, utque aciem partēs dīmittit in omnēs,
vōce, "Venī," magnā clāmat: vocat illa vocantem.
Respicit et rūrsus nūllō veniente, "Quid," inquit
"mē fugis?" et totidem, quot dīxit, verba recēpit.

1. **What was the logic of Juno's punishment of Echo?** (366–369)
2. **How does the description of Echo's condition repeat, with variations, earlier details about her?** (368–369)
3. **What happened to Echo when she saw Narcissus?** (371)
4. **What are the details of the comparison that Ovid uses to describe Echo's pursuit of Narcissus? What do they suggest about her chances of success? How do they make you feel about her?** (372–374)
5. **What does Echo now want to do? To what extent can she carry out her wishes?** (375–377)
6. **How does the conversation between Narcissus and Echo get started? How does it develop? Where are the two speakers in relation to each other?** (377–380)
7. **If the speakers say almost the same words, do they have the same feelings and meanings? How do we know?**
8. **What specific reactions are attributed to Narcissus?** (381–382)
9. **How does a phrase like *nātūra repugnat* apply to the frustrating effect of physical limitations for any human being? How does Ovid want us to feel about such frustration?**

385 **perstō, perstāre** (1), **perstitī, perstātum**, to persist.
alternus, -a, -um, alternate, reciprocal.
dēcipiō, dēcipere (3), **dēcēpī, dēceptum**, to deceive.
386 **coeō, coīre** (*irreg.*), **coīvī, coitum**, to meet, come together. Echo eagerly interprets Narcissus' words in an erotic sense.
libenter, gladly, willingly.
387 **respōnsūra**: future active participle.
388 **verbīs**: what case and why?
ēgredior, ēgredī (3), **ēgressus sum**, to go out, leave. With **silvā**, supply **ē**, "from."
389 **iniciō, inicere** (3), **iniēcī, iniectum**, to throw on, fling upon.
391 **ante . . . quam:** = **antequam**, before.
ēmorior, ēmorī (3), **ēmortuus sum**, to die.
cōpia nostrī: "access to me" (lit., "access to us," but **nostrī** here stands for the singular **meī**).
392 **Sit**: how does Echo change the meaning of the subjunctive?
393 **pudibundus, -a, -um**, ashamed.
394 **prōtegō, prōtegere** (3), **prōtēxī, prōtēctum**, to protect, cover.
ex illō: supply **tempore**.
395 ***dolor, dolōris** (*m*), grief, pain.
repulsa, -ae (*f*), rejection. What kind of genitive?
396 **tenuō** (1), to make thin, weaken. **tenuant . . . cūrae**: frustrated love completes the metamorphosis of the nymph into the Echo that we know, nothing but an answering sound.
vigil, vigilis, wakeful.
***miserābilis, -is, -e**, wretched.
397 **addūcō, addūcere** (3), **addūxī, adductum**, to draw up, wrinkle.
cutis, cutis (*f*), skin.
maciēs, -ēī (*f*), leanness, wasting away.
398 **abeō, abīre** (*irreg.*), **abiī, abitum**, to go away, vanish.
tantum, only.
supersum, superesse (*irreg.*), **superfuī**, to survive.
399 **ferunt**: "they say."
figūra, figūrae (*f*), figure, shape, form.
401 **omnibus**: dative of agent.

402 **aliās**: Ovid turns from Echo back to Narcissus, who, as time passes, disappoints other nymphs.
undīs . . . montibus: ablative of origin.
403 **lūserat**: "tricked" (a verb which inclines us against Narcissus). Notice the pluperfect here and the way Ovid arranges events to focus on the present in lines 415–426.
coetus, -ūs (*m*), group, company.
virīlis, -is, -e, male, masculine.
404 **tollēns**: the gesture of lifting the hands indicates a prayer.
405 **potior, potīrī** (4), **potītus sum**, to possess. This is a curse answering Narcissus' denial of **cōpia** in line 391.
406 **adsentiō, adsentīre** (4), **adsēnsī, adsēnsum**, to agree to. This verb was normally deponent in Ovid's day.
Rhamnūsia, the goddess of divine punishment, Themis or Nemesis, who had a famous temple in Rhamnus near Athens.

III. *Cruel Rejection Provokes a Curse*

Invited to come forward for what promises to be a warm meeting, Echo eagerly does so, only to be rudely spurned by the self-centered Narcissus. In her misery at this rejection, Echo completes her metamorphosis into the bodiless voice that we know.

Perstat et alternae dēceptus imāgine vōcis,
"Hūc coeāmus," ait, nūllīque libentius umquam
respōnsūra sonō, "Coeāmus," rettulit Ēchō,
et verbīs favet ipsa suīs ēgressaque silvā
ībat, ut iniceret spērātō bracchia collō.
Ille fugit fugiēnsque, "Manūs conplexibus aufer!
Ante," ait, "ēmoriar, quam sit tibi cōpia nostrī."
Rettulit illa nihil nisi, "Sit tibi cōpia nostrī."
Sprēta latet silvīs pudibundaque frondibus ōra
prōtegit et sōlīs ex illō vīvit in antrīs;
sed tamen haeret amor crēscitque dolōre repulsae:
et tenuant vigilēs corpus miserābile cūrae,
addūcitque cutem maciēs, et in āera sūcus
corporis omnis abit; vōx tantum atque ossa supersunt:
vōx manet; ossa ferunt lapidis traxisse figūram.
Inde latet silvīs nūllōque in monte vidētur,
omnibus audītur: sonus est, qui vīvit in illā.

When Narcissus spurns others in the same unfeeling manner, the goddess of merited punishment, Nemesis, is invoked to subject him to a similar frustrating experience: to love hopelessly.

Sīc hanc, sīc aliās undīs aut montibus ortās
lūserat hic nymphās, sīc coetūs ante virīlēs;
inde manūs aliquis dēspectus ad aethera tollēns,
"Sīc amet ipse licet, sīc nōn potiātur amātō!"
dīxerat: adsēnsit precibus Rhamnūsia iūstīs.

1. **What confuses Narcissus, and what does he propose?** (385–386)
2. **When Echo repeats Narcissus' words, what does she mean?** (386–387)
3. **How does Echo act on her interpretation of Narcissus' words?** (388–389)
4. **How are Narcissus' reactions to the appearance of Echo expectable for us, but surprising for her?** (390–392)
5. **How does the situation suddenly reverse itself? How is this indicated by Ovid's choice of verbs? Is there any ironic significance in the hunting context?** (389–391)
6. **What does Echo manage to express by her partial repetition of words Narcissus used to reject her?** (392)
7. **What further changes does Echo undergo? How much are her feelings transformed with her body? How does this change affect us differently from the one connected with her earlier punishment by Juno?** (396–401)
8. **What punishment is invoked against Narcissus? Can you guess how it might fit the earlier prophecy? What details has Ovid accumulated to justify this penalty against Narcissus?** (404–406)

407 **inlīmis, -is, -e**, free of mud.
argenteus, -a, -um, silvery.
408 **monte**: again, supply the preposition.
capella, -ae (*f*), she-goat.
409 **volucris** and **fera** (410): both are used as substantives.
410 **turbārat**: = **turbāverat** (which cannot fit the hexameter).
411 **ūmor, ūmōris** (*m*), liquid, water.
412 **passūra**: future active participle with **silva**.
tepēscō, tepēscere (3), **tepēscuī**, to grow warm. In other words, trees shaded the spring.
413 **vēnandī**: gerund. Why the genitive case?
lassus, -a, -um, tired.
414 **prōcumbō, prōcumbere** (3), **prōcubuī, prōcubitum**, to fall forward.
faciem . . . fontem: as the *alliterated* nouns indicate, Narcissus is attracted by the scenery and the water.
415 **dum . . . cupit**: Latin uses the present tense where English requires a continuous past tense.
sēdō (1), to calm, quench.
sitis altera: the second type of thirst is love (for himself).
416 **conripiō, conripere** (3), **conripuī, conreptum**, to seize. As Narcissus leans forward to drink, he notices his own reflection (not, of course, realizing whose it is).
417 **quod . . . est**: relative clause serving as subject of the indirect statement.

418 **adstupeō, adstupēre** (3), **adstupuī** (+ *dat.*), to be amazed (at).
inmōtus, -a, -um, motionless.
419 **Pariō . . . marmore**: Parian marble from the island of Paros was highly prized for its whiteness. We are to think of Narcissus as being almost effeminately white (hence 422, 423), not well tanned (like most hunters).
fōrmō (1), to form, fashion.
signum: in his immobility, Narcissus resembles a statue.
420 **geminum . . . sīdus** and **lūmina**: Ovid here uses astronomical metaphors to refer to the eyes. The metaphors are ironic because Narcissus, on the ground (**humī**), stares only at his reflection, not at the heavens.
421 **dignōs**: with ablative of the gods' names.
crīnis, crīnis (*m*), hair. Both Bacchus, god of wine, and Apollo, god of music and prophecy, were imagined as young males with long hair, like Narcissus.
422 **inpūbēs, inpūbis**, youthful (hence here beardless).
gena, genae (*f*), cheek.
eburneus, -a, -um, ivory, white as ivory.
decus . . . ōris (423): "handsome face."
423 ***candor, candōris** (*m*), whiteness. Ovid and the Romans liked the interplay of red and white.
424 **mīrābilis, -is, -e**, marvelous, amazing. Ovid clarifies the paradox of Narcissus' torment: love demands another person to be loved, but Narcissus cannot get outside himself.
425 **inprūdēns, inprūdentis**, without foresight.
cupit . . . probātur: the verbs of desire and approval are typical of Roman love vocabulary.
426 **petit, petitur . . . accendit et ardet**: note the pairing of verbs, active with passive, transitive with intransitive, to capture the strange way that Narcissus acts on himself.
pariter, equally, simultaneously.

IV. *The Fateful Pool*

In a crystal-clear spring, to which the hot and thirsty boy comes, he leans over to drink, but instead of drinking he becomes totally infatuated with his own irresistible reflection.

Fōns erat inlīmis, nitidīs argenteus undīs,
quem neque pastōrēs neque pastae monte capellae
contigerant aliudve pecus, quem nūlla volucris
nec fera turbārat nec lāpsus ab arbore rāmus;
grāmen erat circā, quod proximus ūmor alēbat,
silvaque sōle locum passūra tepēscere nūllō.
Hic puer et studiō vēnandī lassus et aestū
prōcubuit faciemque locī fontemque secūtus,
dumque sitim sēdāre cupit, sitis altera crēvit,
dumque bibit, vīsae conreptus imāgine fōrmae
spem sine corpore amat, corpus putat esse, quod unda est.

In love, Narcissus acts like any other typical lover. But because he unwittingly desires a reflection of himself, he has no chance of success, for all his efforts.

Adstupet ipse sibī vultūque inmōtus eōdem
haeret ut ē Pariō fōrmātum marmore signum.
Spectat humī positus geminum, sua lūmina, sīdus
et dignōs Bacchō, dignōs et Apolline crīnēs
inpūbēsque genās et eburnea colla decusque
ōris et in niveō mixtum candōre rubōrem
cūnctaque mīrātur, quibus est mīrābilis ipse.
Sē cupit inprūdēns et, quī probat, ipse probātur,
dumque petit, petitur pariterque accendit et ardet.

1. **How is the pool described?** (407–412)
2. **Can you suggest some connections between the details about the pool and Narcissus' character?**
3. **What reasons are given for Narcissus' approach to the pool?** (413–415)
4. **What is the "second thirst" that seizes Narcissus, and what are its causes and symptoms?** (415–417)
5. **How does Ovid convey the futility of Narcissus' love? How is this love both appropriate to his personality and a fitting means of punishing him?** (418–423)
6. **What features of his "beloved" does Narcissus study, and what are his reactions?** (420–424)
7. **How does Ovid suggest the "mirroring" effect in the way he organizes his description? What similarities can you see between the echo (379–392) and reflection (418–426) sequences?**
8. **What interest does the Ovidian narrator have in this situation, and how does he control our reactions to Narcissus? Are we supposed to feel sympathy or some other sentiment?** (425–426)

427 **inritus, -a, -um**, futile, empty.
428 **in mediīs** . . . **aquīs** (429): artfully interlocked word order suggests the confusion of boy and reflection. A revised order that might help an English translation would be: **quotiēns bracchia captantia collum vīsum in mediīs aquīs**.
429 **illīs**: i.e., **aquīs**.
430 **quid videat** . . . **quod videt**: explain the different syntax of these two clauses.
431 ***error, errōris** (*m*), mistake, error. Narcissus is now deceived by a reflection as earlier (385) by an echo.
432 **crēdulus, -a, -um**, credulous, gullible.
fugācia: note the theme of flight throughout this story (384, 456, 477), the fugitive being a beloved, rather than a hunted animal.
captō (1), to chase, try to catch.
433 **avertere**: "turn away" (imperative). Ovid has compressed his structure to put the three verbs together.
434 **repercutiō, repercutere** (3), **repercussī, repercussum**, to strike back, reflect. Narcissus is emphatically told that he merely sees the "shadow of a reflection."
435 **vēnitque manetque**: the double **-que** is an imitation of a device of Homeric Greek epic. Translate only the second **-que**.
436 **discēdet** . . . **possīs**: what is the effect here of the mixed condition?

437 **illum**: Narcissus, who pays no attention to the apostrophe of the poet.
***Cereris**: Ceres, divine giver of grain to mankind, here stands for food in general. The use of a god's name to refer to his or her area of activity is known as *antonomasia*.
438 **fūsus**: "sprawled," "collapsed." The grass around the spring was mentioned in line 411.
439 **inexplētus, -a, -um**, unsatisfied.
mendāx, mendācis, lying, deceptive. Ovid regularly suggests in this poem that physical form is deceptive. Even more unreliable are reflections of forms.
lūmine: cf. **sua lūmina** (420).
440 **perit**: Ovid emphasizes the paradox of Narcissus' foolish love: he dies "through" or because of his own eyes.
441 **tendēns sua bracchia**: as Narcissus gets ready to make a long speech, Ovid assigns him a dramatic gesture somewhat like that in line 404, but different in significance: the boy appeals for sympathy from nonhuman nature (ironic for one who has proved so indifferent to other human beings).
442 **Ecquis**: "Is there anyone who?"
***crūdēlius**, more cruelly. "Cruel love" is an old theme.
443 **latebra**: Narcissus alludes to the fact that the woods have always been a favorite place for making love.
444 **saecula**: nominative subject.
445 **quī** . . . **tābuerit**: the antecedent of **quī** is **ecquem** (444).
tābēscō, tābēscere (3), **tābuī**, to waste away. **tābuerit**: perfect subjunctive in relative clause of characteristic.
446 **quod**: object of the first and subject of the second of the two verbs.

V. *Mirror Effects*

When the poet has described the irrational acts and feelings of this self-love, he intervenes and addresses his character Narcissus, trying, of course in vain, to bring him to his senses.

Inrita fallācī quotiēns dedit ōscula fontī!
In mediīs quotiēns vīsum captantia collum
bracchia mersit aquīs nec sē dēprendit in illīs!
Quid videat, nescit, sed, quod videt, ūritur illō
atque oculōs īdem, quī dēcipit, incitat error.
Crēdule, quid frūstrā simulacra fugācia captās?
Quod petis, est nusquam; quod amās, avertere, perdēs.
Ista repercussae, quam cernis, imāginis umbra est:
nīl habet ista suī: tēcum vēnitque manetque,
tēcum discēdet, sī tū discēdere possīs.

Deaf to advice, indifferent to food and sleep, Narcissus continues to stare fondly at his reflection. He then launches into a pathetic speech and appeals to the sympathy of the surrounding woods.

Nōn illum Cereris, nōn illum cūra quiētis
abstrahere inde potest, sed opācā fūsus in herbā
spectat inexplētō mendācem lūmine fōrmam
perque oculōs perit ipse suōs paulumque levātus,
ad circumstantēs tendēns sua bracchia silvās,
"Ecquis, iō silvae, crūdēlius," inquit, "amāvit?
Scītis enim et multīs latebra opportūna fuistis.
Ecquem, cum vestrae tot agantur saecula vītae,
quī sīc tābuerit, longō meministis in aevō?
Et placet et videō, sed, quod videōque placetque,
nōn tamen inveniō: tantus tenet error amantem!

1. **What does Narcissus do when he sees the reflection of his neck? Is he successful in his action? What would presumably happen to the reflection?** (428–429)
2. **How does water make a much more frustrating mirror than the solid polished surfaces that people usually employ?**
3. **How does Ovid define Narcissus' confusion? In what ways does the boy misinterpret what he sees?** (430–431)
4. **What does Ovid achieve by *apostrophizing*, i.e., by introducing and addressing Narcissus directly? Are his words primarily for Narcissus or for the reader? What tone seems to emerge—sympathy, impatience, instruction, or what?** (432–436)
5. **When Ovid returns to describing Narcissus, does the boy show changes that suggest he has responded to Ovid's advice? What exactly is he doing?** (437–439)
6. **Is it only a figure of speech that Narcissus is perishing? How do you know?** (440)
7. **What kind of audience does Narcissus have for his speech? In what ways is it appropriate to the speaker and situation?** (441)
8. **What ambiguity do you detect in Narcissus' first question?** (442) **What does he mean by "cruel loving"? What other sense of "cruel loving" applies to Narcissus' earlier behavior?**
9. **How had the woods proved convenient, according to Narcissus?** (443)
10. **Is there an answer to Narcissus' rhetorical question about wasting away that differs from what he expects? Who else has wasted away?** (444–445)
11. **How does Narcissus now describe his *error* (447)? Does it have aspects different from its sense in line 431?**

448 **Quōque**: = **Et quō**, introducing a relative clause of purpose.
sēparō (1), to separate, divide. Lovers' separation is a common pathetic theme in Latin poetry.
449 **clausīs . . . portīs**: ablative of means.
450 **Cupit ipse**: Narcissus sees his own desires reflected but believes that the image projects an independent passion that responds to his.
451 ***porrigō, porrigere** (3), **porrēxī, porrēctum**, to extend, offer. **porrēximus**: editorial "we" (cf. **nostrī**, 391).
lympha, lymphae (*f*), water.
452 **resupīnus, -a, -um**, bent back, lying back.
453 **posse . . . tangī**: **hunc** is implied as the subject of the indirect statement.
obstō, obstāre (1), **obstitī, obstātum** (+ *dat.*), to stand in the way of, hinder.
455 **-ve**, or.
456 **fugiās**: why subjunctive?

457 **nescio quam**: "some" (lit., "I do not know what"). The two words function as an adjective.
prōmittō, prōmittere (3), prōmīsī, prōmissum, to promise.
amīcō: here, an adjective rather than noun.
458 **porrēxī**: Narcissus starts to list some of his movements that are mirrored in the water.
460 **mē lacrimante**, ablative absolute.
lacrimō (1), to cry, weep.
461 **quantum**: "as."
462 **verba refers**: since he is speaking as he looks at his reflection, Narcissus thinks it speaks.
463 **Iste ego sum**: here, the opening prophecy (348) is fulfilled.
464 **ūror**: cf. **ūritur** (430).
meī: genitive of **ego**; why does Ovid use this word instead of the possessive adjective?
465 **Quid faciam? . . . Quid . . . rogābō?**: the questions imply helpless desperation.
466 **inops, inopis**, needy, destitute. Ovid deliberately places **inopem** near the word **cōpia**, its opposite in sense. Remember, Narcissus denied that same **cōpia** to Echo (391).

VI. *The Lover's Delusions*

From the way the reflection "echoes" Narcissus' passionate looks and gestures, he irrationally infers that his love is shared and returned. Then he starts to address the reflection itself.

Quōque magis doleam, nec nōs mare sēparat ingēns
nec via nec montēs nec clausīs moenia portīs:
exiguā prohibēmur aquā! Cupit ipse tenērī!
Nam quotiēns liquidīs porrēximus ōscula lymphīs,
hic totiēns ad mē resupīnō nītitur ōre;
posse putēs tangī: minimum est, quod amantibus obstat.
Quisquis es, hūc exī! Quid mē, puer ūnice, fallis
quōve petītus abīs? Certē nec fōrma nec aetās
est mea, quam fugiās, et amārunt mē quoque nymphae.

Momentarily Narcissus finds reason to hope, but the mirroring of his actions makes him finally realize that he and his "beloved" are one and the same person. He faces an impossible situation, which he cannot rationally handle.

Spem mihi nescio quam vultū prōmittis amīcō,
cumque ego porrēxī tibi bracchia, porrigis ultrō;
cum rīsī, adrīdēs; lacrimās quoque saepe notāvī
mē lacrimante tuās; nūtū quoque signa remittis
et, quantum mōtū fōrmōsī suspicor ōris,
verba refers aurēs nōn pervenientia nostrās.
Iste ego sum! sēnsī; nec mē mea fallit imāgō:
ūror amōre meī, flammās moveōque ferōque.
Quid faciam? Roger, anne rogem? Quid deinde rogābō?
Quod cupiō, mēcum est: inopem mē cōpia fēcit.

1. **How does the separation of Narcissus and his beloved differ from the usual "lovers' separation"? How does Narcissus feel about the situation?** (448–450)
2. **Why does Narcissus believe that his beloved is eager to answer his passion? What would happen, however, as their lips met?** (451–453)
3. **Is Narcissus right to claim that only a slight obstacle interferes with the lovers? What does he mean? What is the truth?** (453)
4. **In addressing his reflection as *puer ūnice*, how does Narcissus unwittingly express the ambiguity of this whole situation?** (454)
5. **Why does Narcissus think it odd that his beloved suddenly disappears? What experience proves to him that lovers would not avoid him?** (455–456)
6. **How has the reflection given him reason to hope?** (457)
7. **What actions of Narcissus does the reflection repeat? How do these reflected motions of affection serve as a just punishment for Narcissus' refusal to let Echo turn his neutral words into love?** (458–460)
8. **Since words cannot be reflected but only echoed, what does Narcissus suspect about his beloved's response to his own verbal appeals? Why?** (460–462)
9. **When he finally grasps his predicament, in how many ways does Narcissus express this realization?** (463–464)
10. **How does Narcissus summarize his plight in terms of a paradoxical *cōpia?*** (466) **How does that remind us both of his rejection of Echo in line 391 and of the curse invoked against him in line 405?**

467 **sēcēdō, sēcēdere** (3), **sēcessī, sēcessum**, to withdraw, retire, escape.

468 **vōtum, -ī** (*n*), prayer, vow. **vōtum in amante novum**: "a strange prayer by a lover" (to introduce what follows).

vellem: supply **ut**, "I wish that."

470 **prīmō . . . in aevō**: "in the prime of life."

extinguō, extinguere (3), **extinxī, extinctum**, to put out, extinguish, destroy.

471 **mihi**: dative of reference, modified by **positūrō** (which has its own clause).

472 **vellem**: **ut** is omitted as in line 468.

diuturnus, -a, -um, long lasting. A lover regularly wishes to be survived by the beloved.

473 **concordēs**: to be united in death usually symbolizes perfect love, but here it emphasizes the paradox of the situation.

474 **rediit**: after vain appeals to the trees, to his reflection, and to us, Narcissus turns back to the pool and its image.

male sānus: = **īnsānus**.

475 **turbāvit**: his tears trouble the waters which no bird or beast (cf. 410) had troubled; as a result the reflection is troubled.

477 **crūdēlis**: Narcissus again addresses the reflection (cf. 454–462).

478 **quod . . . est**: object of **adspicere** (479).

479 **alimentum, -ī** (*n*), food, nourishment. The madness of love is "hunger" here, as earlier (415) it was "thirst."

480 **ōra, -ae** (*f*), shore, boundary, edge. Narcissus ripped his robe down from the top and bared his chest.

481 **nūda . . . pectora palmīs**: this arrangement of adjectives and nouns around a central verb (AAVNN) was known as a "Golden Line." Ovid enhances it here by alliteration of the letter *p*.

marmoreus, -a, -um, of marble, white as marble. Ovid reminds us of his earlier statue simile (419).

percutiō, percutere (3), **percussī, percussum**, to strike.

482 **roseus, -a, -um**, rosy, reddish. Ovid aims for the pretty mixture of white (arms) and rosy (chest, after being struck), as in line 423.

483 **nōn aliter quam**: for a similar start to a simile, cf. line 373.

parte: ablative of respect, "in part," "partly."

484 **racēmus, -ī** (*m*), cluster.

485 **purpureum**: the reddish color of unripe, ripening grapes, not the dark purple of those ready for picking.

486 **Quae**: i.e., **pectora**. Narcissus sees the image of what Ovid has so sensuously described for us.

488 **mātūtīnus, -a, -um**, of the morning, early.

pruīna, -ae (*f*), frost.

489 **attenuātus**: Narcissus wastes away as Echo did earlier (396).

490 **līquor, līquī** (3) (*only in present tense*), to be or become liquid, melt.

carpitur: "is devoured" (same image as in line 479).

VII. *The Lover Embraces Death*

Narcissus accepts, even welcomes the necessity of death, comforted by the thought that at least, unlike other tragic lovers, he will die "with" his beloved. In death they will finally be united.

Ō utinam ā nostrō sēcēdere corpore possem!
Vōtum in amante novum: vellem, quod amāmus, abesset!
Iamque dolor vīrēs adimit, nec tempora vītae
longa meae superant, prīmōque extinguor in aevō.
Nec mihi mors gravis est, positūrō morte dolōrēs:
hic, quī dīligitur, vellem, diuturnior esset!
Nunc duo concordēs animā moriēmur in ūnā."
Dīxit et ad faciem rediit male sānus eandem
et lacrimīs turbāvit aquās, obscūraque mōtō
reddita fōrma lacū est. Quam cum vīdisset abīre,
"Quō refugis? Remanē nec mē, crūdēlis, amantem
dēsere," clāmāvit. "Liceat, quod tangere nōn est,
adspicere et miserō praebēre alimenta furōrī!"

Narcissus beats and bruises his chest in self-pity, the sight of which in his reflection sends him into paroxysms of remorse. He then begins to waste away.

Dumque dolet, summā vestem dēdūxit ab ōrā
nūdaque marmoreīs percussit pectora palmīs.
Pectora traxērunt roseum percussa rubōrem,
nōn aliter quam pōma solent, quae candida parte,
parte rubent, aut ut variīs solet ūva racēmīs
dūcere purpureum nōndum mātūra colōrem.
Quae simul adspexit liquefactā rūrsus in undā,
nōn tulit ulterius, sed, ut intābēscere flāvae
igne levī cērae mātūtīnaeque pruīnae
sōle tepente solent, sīc attenuātus amōre
līquitur et tēctō paulātim carpitur ignī.

1. **What strange new wish does Narcissus express?** (467–468)
2. **Why does he think he is dying? Why does he find death acceptable?** (469–471)
3. **What will happen to his beloved reflection that he regrets?** (472–473)
4. **What happens when he starts crying?** (475–476)
5. **How much understanding of the situation does Narcissus' speech to his reflection show?** (477–479) **Compare what he said at 454–460.**
6. **How does Narcissus show his pained feelings?** (480–481)
7. **To what does Ovid compare Narcissus' beaten chest? How do the comparisons affect the reader?** (482–485)
8. **How is Narcissus affected by the reflection's suffering?** (486–487)
9. **How does the fire image work in the description of Narcissus' symptoms?** (487–490) **Do the comparisons produce sympathy for the boy? Do they distance us, or do they merely emphasize the fantastic aspects of the story?**

491 **color**: the colors of Narcissus' "ripening" body fade out.
492 **vīrēs, vīrium** (*f pl*), strength. **vigor et vīrēs**: "vim and vigor."
494 **Quae**: i.e., Echo.
quamvīs (*used with indicative by Ovid*), although.
495 **indolēscō, indolēscere** (3), **indoluī**, to grieve, feel sorry.
***ēheu**, alas.
496 **resonus, -a, -um**, resounding, echoing.
iterō (1), to repeat.
497 **lacertus, -ī** (*m*), upper arm.
498 **sonitus, -ūs** (*m*), noise, sound.
plangor, plangōris (*m*), beating, striking. Echo's special sympathy is more than verbal in this case.
499 **solitus, -a, -um**, accustomed, usual. With **undam**.
spectantis: "of the one looking."
500 **Heu frustrā dīlēcte puer**: the full irony of the situation emerges: what Narcissus says to his unanswering reflection perfectly matches what Echo can say in grief over his failure to answer her love.
501 **dictōque Valē**: ablative absolute (the imperative **valē** takes the place of a noun in the ablative case).
"Vale" inquit: although grammar requires the second **valē** to have final long *e* like the first, Ovid shortens (does *not* elide) the *e* before **inquit**. Thus, echoed **vale** trails off at the end. Vergil had earlier produced a similar effect in *Eclogue* III.79.

503 **lūmina . . . fōrmam**: in English word order: **mors clausit lūmina mīrantia fōrmam dominī**. As he dies, Narcissus is still gazing raptly at his reflection.
504 **īnfernus, -a, -um**, infernal. Narcissus has gone down to the world of the dead.
505 **Stygius, -a, -um**, of the Styx (the most famous of the rivers of the underworld).
***plangō, plangere** (3), **planxī, planctum**, to beat one's breast.
506 **nāis, nāidis** (*f*), naiad, water nymph.
secō, secāre (1), **secuī, sectum**, to cut. Cutting locks of hair and dedicating them to the dead was a mark of grief.
507 **dryadēs, dryadum** (*f pl*), wood nymphs.
plangentibus: the last we hear of Echo, she is trying to match the grief of the nymphs, since she can no longer respond to the dead and silent Narcissus.
508 **rogum, -ī** (*n*), funeral pyre.
quatiō, quatere (3), ———, **quassum**, to shake, brandish.
feretrum, -ī (*n*), bier, litter. All these preparations prove useless: nothing is left of the once-beautiful body.
509 **croceus, -a, -um**, yellow, golden. The word order obliges us to take **croceum** with **flōrem**, but then it turns out that the "flower" is surrounded by white petals.

VIII. *Self-Admiration to the End*

Echo who, despite Narcissus' cruel indifference, has remained sympathetic to him, returns to pity the dying boy. As he laments his pathetic love for "another," she is able to respond and express her own fond regret.

Et neque iam color est mixtō candōre rubōrī
nec vigor et vīrēs et quae modo vīsa placēbant,
nec corpus remanet, quondam quod amāverat Ēchō.
Quae tamen ut vīdit, quamvīs īrāta memorque
indoluit, quotiēnsque puer miserābilis, "Ēheu,"
dīxerat, haec resonīs iterābat vōcibus, "Ēheu."
Cumque suōs manibus percusserat ille lacertōs,
haec quoque reddēbat sonitum plangōris eundem.
Ultima vōx solitam fuit haec spectantis in undam:
"Heu frūstrā dīlēcte puer!" totidemque remīsit
verba locus, dictōque Valē "Vale" inquit et Ēchō.

Narcissus dies and descends to the underworld, where he continues to admire his reflection in the river Styx. He leaves behind no corpse for a funeral, but instead a pretty, though soulless, flower.

Ille caput viridī fessum submīsit in herbā,
lūmina mors clausit dominī mīrantia fōrmam.
Tum quoque sē, postquam est īnfernā sēde receptus,
in Stygiā spectābat aquā. Planxēre sorōrēs
nāides et sectōs frātrī posuēre capillōs,
planxērunt dryadēs: plangentibus adsonat Ēchō.
Iamque rogum quassāsque facēs feretrumque parābant:
nusquam corpus erat, croceum prō corpore flōrem
inveniunt foliīs medium cingentibus albīs.

1. **In what respects is Narcissus no longer like the sturdy young man of the story's opening?** (491–493)
2. **How does Ovid reintroduce Echo? Why is it appropriate that she should especially regret the loss of *corpus?*** (493)
3. **What mixture of feelings characterizes Echo?** (494–495)
4. **How does Echo now echo Narcissus? How does the situation and her response differ from before?** (495–498)
5. **What are Narcissus' last words? How do we respond to them? How, on the contrary, do we feel about Echo and her repetitions?** (499–501)
6. **To what extent do the words *frūstrā dīlēcte puer* (500) summarize the complex theme of Ovid's story?**
7. **Where does Narcissus lay his head? What significance does the detail about his eyes have in controlling our sympathies?** (502–503)
8. **When Narcissus goes down to Hades, to what extent does his behavior change as the result of death?** (504–505)
9. **How do the nymphs show their grief for Narcissus? Who else participates and how?** (505–507)
10. **What funeral preparations are made? What happened to the funeral?** (508–509)
11. **Where was Narcissus' corpse? How does Ovid describe the flower? What is the reader's response to this metamorphosis? How might Ovid have guaranteed our sympathy and regret, if he had wanted them?** (509–510)

PENTHEUS

Death of Pentheus, Pompeii (the House of the Vetti)

511 **Cognita rēs**: "The story when known." The tragedy of Narcissus, as predicted by Tiresias, should have influenced Pentheus not to despise the prophet. There are echoes in the words **vātēs** and **augur** of lines 348–349.

Achāidas: "Greek." In fact, the geographical focus moves but a short distance in Boeotia from the region of the River Cephisos to the city of Thebes.

512 **attulerat . . . erat**: Ovid's tenses, pluperfect and imperfect, prepare for the presents of the main narrative in the next lines.

513 **Echīonidēs**: i.e., Pentheus, son of Echion and (as we will learn in line 725) of Agave. He inherited the rule in Thebes from his grandfather Cadmus, who had founded the city.

hunc: i.e., Tiresias. Rejection of wise advice or warnings serves as tragic foreshadowing. Cf. our common expressions: "Mark my words" and "I told you so." Note how the story defines Pentheus as unique in his arrogant folly.

514 **contemptor, contemptōris** (*m*), despiser. The noun appeared in epic, used for another arrogant disbeliever, Mezentius, in Vergil's *Aeneid* VII.648.

superum: = **superōrum** (contracted gen. pl.), "of the gods above."

praesāgus, -a, -um, foreboding, prophetic.

515 **senis**: i.e., the old Tiresias.

tenebrās: i.e., the "darkness" of Tiresias' blindness, which will motivate the paradoxical prediction that follows.

clādes, clādis (*f*), disaster, loss.

lūcis adēmptae: "of (his) lost light (= eyesight)."

516 **obiciō, obicere** (3), **obiēcī, obiectum**, to throw in one's face, taunt with. Mocking a disability is an act of basic cruelty, for Ovid's audience as well as for us.

Ille: i.e., Tiresias.

albeō, albēre (2), to be white. Ovid sets up an effective contrast between age and youth as well as between pious prophet and blasphemer.

517 **essēs . . . fierēs** (518) **. . . vidērēs**: explain the subjunctives.

518 **orbus, -a, -um**, deprived of. With genitive, **lūminis huius** (517).

Bacchicus, -a, -um, of Bacchus. Ovid here introduces the role of Pentheus' divine adversary and destroyer, Bacchus. For the fatal scene where Pentheus sees the forbidden Bacchic rites, see below lines 710–731.

519 **diēs . . . quam**: note the feminine gender.

auguror, augurārī (1), **augurātus sum**, to act as augur (cf. 512), prophesy.

520 **veniat**: subjunctive in clause of characteristic.

Semelēius, -a, -um, of Semele. She was a princess of Thebes, aunt of Pentheus. She died after conceiving Bacchus by Jupiter.

Līber: i.e., Bacchus, the "liberating" god of wine.

521 **dignor, dignārī** (1), **dignātus sum** (+ *abl.*), to treat as worthy.

522 **lacer, lacera, lacerum**, torn apart.

spargēre: 2nd person singular future passive (= **spargēris**).

523 **foedō** (1), to defile, pollute. Pentheus will be torn to pieces by his mother and aunts, who thereby will be defiled.

524 **dignābere**: = **dignāberis**. Cf. note on **spargēre** (522).

nūmen: i.e., the divine power of Bacchus.

525 **querēris**: "you will lament." Pentheus will admit with regret that Tiresias really did "see" the future.

526 **Echīone nātus**: cf. **Echīonidēs** (513).

527 **fidēs sequitur**: the narrator now moves into the main situation, announcing that events prove Tiresias right.

respōnsum, -ī (*n*), answer.

aguntur: "are worked out."

528 ***ululātus, -ūs** (*m*), howl, wailing (especially of women).

529 **mixtae**: fem. nom. pl., agreeing with the two nouns at the end of the line. The verb can take **cum** + ablative or simple dative.

nurus, -ūs (*f*), daughter-in-law.

530 **procerēs, procerum** (*m pl*), leading men.

ignōta . . . sacra: the rites are unknown because they are new, connected with a hitherto unknown deity.

OVID, *METAMORPHOSES* III.511–733

I. *Pentheus Challenges Fate*

The true prophecy about Narcissus stirs the contemptuous doubts of the Theban ruler, young Pentheus. To him the same prophet Tiresias predicts a terrible death when he refuses to honor the god Bacchus.

Cognita rēs meritam vātī per Achāidas urbēs
attulerat fāmam, nōmenque erat auguris ingēns.
Spernit Echīonidēs tamen hunc ex omnibus ūnus,
contemptor superum Pentheus, praesāgaque rīdet
verba senis tenebrāsque et clādem lūcis adēmptae
ōbicit. Ille movēns albentia tempora cānīs
"Quam fēlīx essēs, sī tū quoque lūminis huius
orbus," ait, "fierēs, nē Bacchica sacra vidērēs.
Namque diēs aderit, quam nōn procul auguror esse,
quā novus hūc veniat, prōlēs Semelēia, Līber;
quem nisi templōrum fueris dignātus honōre,
mīlle lacer spargēre locīs et sanguine silvās
foedābis mātremque tuam mātrisque sorōrēs.
Ēveniet. Neque enim dignābere nūmen honōre,
mēque sub hīs tenebrīs nimium vīdisse querēris."

Pentheus spurns such ominous warnings. When Bacchus does arrive and the rest of the Thebans welcome his advent with heartfelt celebrations of his rites, Pentheus in his outrage harangues them.

Tālia dīcentem prōturbat Echīone nātus.
Dicta fidēs sequitur, respōnsaque vātis aguntur.
Līber adest, fēstīsque fremunt ululātibus agrī:
turba ruit, mixtaeque virīs mātrēsque nurūsque
vulgusque procerēsque ignōta ad sacra feruntur.

1. **What had Tiresias earned?** (511–512)
2. **How is Pentheus exceptional in his attitude?** (513)
3. **In what ways does Pentheus ridicule Tiresias?** (514–516)
4. **What paradox does Tiresias express in his response?** (517–518) **How does this paradox remind you of Tiresias' prophecy about Narcissus in lines 346–348?**
5. **How does Tiresias elaborate this paradox in lines 519–523? How does he explain why blindness would be preferable?**
6. **On the basis of lines 522–523, what do you think is going to happen to Pentheus and his female relatives?**
7. **How do Tiresias' final remarks return to the point from which he started?** (524–525)
8. **Does the narrator side with Tiresias? How can we tell that Pentheus is wrong and that Tiresias is right?** (526–527)
9. **What event seems to confirm the initial details of Tiresias' prophecy?** (528)
10. **How do all the other Thebans respond to Liber's arrival?** (529–530) **On the basis of the story so far, how do you expect Pentheus to act?**

531 **anguigenae**: "snake-born" (voc. pl.). Most of the Thebans are descendants of the "dragon seed," the men who sprang from the soil when Cadmus planted the teeth of the dragon he had killed as it guarded the terrain. Pentheus' own father Echion was one of the snake-born. The Greek word *echis* means "snake."

Māvortius, -a, -um, of Mars. The dragon was a creature of Mars, the war god, and so the Thebans in their turn become "children of Mars." The phrase should remind Ovid's Roman audience of their own legendary origin in connection with Mars, father of Romulus and Remus and sponsor of the wolf that nursed them. Ovid ironically makes his unappealing Pentheus sound the conservative notes of Roman political rhetoric.

532 **attonō, attonāre** (1), **attonuī, attonitum**, to strike with a thunderbolt, dumbfound, astonish.

Aera: the bronze here is that of cymbals, used in the emotional dances for Bacchus.

533 **repulsus, -a, -um**, struck against, smashed.

aduncus, -a, -um, curved, hooked. **aduncō . . . cornū**: ablative of description with **tībia**. The pipes, usually made from wood or reeds, here are of animal horn.

tībia, -ae (*f*), pipe, flute.

534 **magicus, -a, -um**, magical. A typical disbeliever, Pentheus sneers at religious frenzy as "tricks."

535 **tuba, -ae** (*f*), curved war trumpet. Pentheus recalls the Thebans' martial heritage in Roman terms.

strīctus, -a, -um (*perfect passive participle from* **stringō**), drawn. **strīctīs . . . tēlīs**: ablative of description with **agmina**.

536 **īnsānia, -ae** (*f*), madness. The word characterizes Pentheus' prejudices more than it does the behavior of the Thebans.

vīnō: ablative of means. Wine of course alludes to the typical power of Bacchus.

537 **obscēnus, -a, -um**, ill-omened, filthy, indecent.

tympanum, -ī (n), drum (which has a hollow, reverberating area, hence **inānia**).

538 **mīrer**: deliberative subjunctive.

vectus: perfect passive participle of **vehō**, "carried." In theory, Pentheus is addressing the few old companions (not "snake-born") of Cadmus who came with him from Tyre. They resemble the companions of Aeneas who came to Italy across the sea.

539 **hāc**: with **sēde**, ablative of place where.

Tyron: Greek accusative of **Tyros** (nominative); Tyre, a city of Phoenicia, was ruled by Cadmus' father, Agenor.

profugus, -a, -um, fugitive. This was a characteristic Vergilian word for the Trojan refugees who founded Roman civilization. Ovid has transferred the word to the household gods or Penates (exploiting alliteration).

540 **Marte**: referring both to Thebes' (and Rome's) patron deity and to his main activity of warfare.

capī: Pentheus raves as though Thebes has been tamely captured by this alien ("enemy") superstition.

542 **thyrsus, -ī** (*m*), staff (used by Bacchus' followers) entwined with a garland and tipped with a pine cone. Pentheus invidiously contrasts the gear of Bacchic worship with that of war.

543 **Este**: imperative of **sum**. **stirps, stirpis** (*f*), stem, stock.

544 **illīus**: with **serpentis** in line 545. Before Cadmus killed it, the serpent killed many of his Tyrian followers.

545 **Prō fontibus**: Pentheus perversely presents the monster as "heroic defender" of local waters.

546 **intereō, interīre** (*irreg.*), **interiī, interitum**, to die. The "heroic death" should impel the Thebans to heroic combat and victory.

547 **lētum, -ī** (*n*), death.

mollēs: "effeminate." Typical male sneer against opponents.

548 **patrius, -a, -um**, father's, ancestral. Pentheus foolishly links patriotism to the dragon.

vetābant: the imperfect indicative can serve in contrary-to-fact conditions, as here.

549 **Thēbae, -ārum** (*f pl*), Thebes. **tormentum, -ī** (*n*), war engine, sling artillery.

550 **dīruō, dīruere** (3), **dīruī, dīrutum**, to destroy.

II. *Pentheus the Rabid Patriot*

Pentheus appeals to the martial heritage of his people (as if they were Romans) against what he denounces as the soft, effeminate allure of Bacchus.

"Quis furor, anguigenae, prōlēs Māvortia, vestrās
attonuit mentēs?" Pentheus ait. "Aerane tantum
aere repulsa valent et aduncō tībia cornū
et magicae fraudēs, ut, quōs nōn bellicus ēnsis,
nōn tuba terruerit, nōn strictīs agmina tēlīs,
fēmineae vōcēs et mōta īnsānia vīnō
obscēnīque gregēs et inānia tympana vincant?
Vōsne, senēs, mīrer, quī longa per aequora vectī
hāc Tyron, hāc profugōs posuistis sēde Penātēs,
nunc sinitis sine Marte capī? Vōsne, ācrior aetās
ō iuvenēs, propiorque meae, quōs arma tenēre,
nōn thyrsōs, galeāque tegī, nōn fronde decēbat?

The king further reminds the Thebans that they are descended from the dragon that died defending their land against an armed invader: they should imitate its heroic behavior.

Este, precor, memorēs, quā sītis stirpe creātī,
illīusque animōs, quī multōs perdidit ūnus,
sūmite serpentis. Prō fontibus ille lacūque
interiit: at vōs prō fāmā vincite vestrā.
Ille dedit lētō fortēs, vōs pellite mollēs
et patrium retinēte decus. Sī fāta vetābant
stāre diū Thēbās, utinam tormenta virīque
moenia dīruerent, ferrumque ignisque sonārent.

1. **What madness does Pentheus protest against? To what extent is he right from his viewpoint?** (531–534)
2. **How does Ovid manipulate the reader's response to Pentheus' appeal to a martial ancestry?** (534–535)
3. **What details does Pentheus fix on to characterize the practices of Bacchic worship?** (536–537)
4. **What makes Pentheus so indignant over this Bacchic "conquest"?**
5. **How in Pentheus' view have the old men betrayed their past deeds?** (538–540)
6. **How have the young men also gone wrong in Pentheus' view?** (540–542)
7. **What does Pentheus want them to do as true patriots?** (541–542)
8. **What kind of model does the Thebans' dragon-ancestor provide?** (543–546)
9. **Why does Pentheus consider the Thebans' present task easier than that of their ancestor?** (547–548) **Is it?**
10. **How does Ovid expect the reader to react to Pentheus' view of this ancestor of the Thebans?**
11. **If Thebes had to collapse, how would Pentheus want it to go?** (549–550)

551 **Essēmus**: Pentheus continues rhetorically with his contrary-to-fact situation: defeated in war, the Thebans would be wretched but not ashamed (as in his view they should feel disgraced now). The gerundives **querenda** . . . **cēlanda** (552) reinforce the contrast of grief and disgrace.
552 **cēlō** (1), to conceal, hide.
foret: = **esset**.
553 **inermis, -is, -e**, unarmed. Bacchus is contemptuously dismissed as a "boy."
555 **madidus, -a, -um**, wet, drenched.
murra, -ae (*f*), myrrh, used as hair ointment.
556 **pingō, pingere** (3), **pinxī, pictum**, to paint.
intexō, intexere (3), **intexuī, intextum**, to weave in. The two lists in lines 554–556 again contrast the effeminate and the warrior.
557 **Quem**: i.e., the "boy" Bacchus.
āctūtum (*adv.*), immediately.
absistō, absistere (3), **abstitī**, to stand aside, withdraw.
558 **adsumptum**: "falsely assumed."
commentus, -a, -um, feigned, fictitious.
559 **Ācrisiō**: Acrisius, king of Argos, regularly viewed as a villain because of his cruelty to his daughter Danae and his grandson Perseus. No other ancient source refers to his opposition to Bacchus, but we may be sure that Ovid's audience is to regard Acrisius as no more of a heroic model than the Theban snake cited earlier by Pentheus.
animī: partitive genitive with **satis**.
contemnere . . . **claudere** (560): the infinitives express result after **satis** . . . **est** (also expressible with **ut** + subjunctive).
560 **Argolicus, -a, -um**, of Argos.
venientī: dative of reference applying to Bacchus, who came as an outsider to Argos, as now (cf. 528) to Thebes.
561 **advena, -ae** (*m*), newcomer.
562 **famulīs** . . . **imperat**: Ovid likes parenthetical remarks that can serve as "stage directions."
563 **abestō**: 3rd person singular future imperative, "let (it) be absent."

564 **avus, -ī** (*m*), grandfather. I.e., Cadmus.
Athamās: the husband of Ino, a daughter of Cadmus.
565 **inhibeō, inhibēre** (2), **inhibuī, inhibitum**, to restrain, check. It is a common narrative device to depict a man's rashness by showing the inability of wiser men to control him.
566 **admonitus, -ūs** (*m*), warning, advice.
inrītō (1), to stir up, stimulate.
567 **moderāmen, moderāminis** (*n*), control, restraint.
nocēbant: "were making it (or him) worse."
568 **sīc ego** . . . **vīdī** (569): Ovid now introduces what purports to be a firsthand observation, which functions as a simile. The Italian springtime torrent was and is a common phenomenon.
euntī: dative depending on **obstābat** and referring to the torrent.
569 **modicus, -a, -um**, moderate, slight.
570 **quācumque**, wherever.
obstruō, obstruere (3), **obstruxī, obstructum** (+ *dat.*), to block, hinder.
tenēbant: supply **torrentem** as direct object.
571 **spumeus, -a, -um**, foaming, frothy. This and the other adjectives in this line apply figuratively to the violent reactions of Pentheus.

III. *Violence Against Bacchus' New Religion*

Filled with a sense of national disgrace, Pentheus turns his fury against the god Bacchus, whose divinity he categorically denies. Voicing ferocious threats, he impiously orders his slaves to capture and bind the ringleader of these rites and bring him into his presence.

"Essēmus miserī sine crīmine, sorsque querenda,
nōn cēlanda foret, lacrimaeque pudōre carērent:
at nunc ā puerō Thēbae capientur inermī,
quem neque bella iuvant nec tēla nec ūsus equōrum,
sed madidus murrā crīnis mollēsque corōnae
purpuraque et pictīs intextum vestibus aurum.
Quem quidem ego āctūtum (modo vōs absistite) cōgam
adsumptumque patrem commentaque sacra fatērī.
An satis Ācrisiō est animī contemnere vānum
nūmen et Argolicās venientī claudere portās,
Penthea terrēbit cum tōtīs advena Thēbīs?
Īte citī"—famulīs hoc imperat—"Īte ducemque
attrahite hūc vinctum. Iussīs mora segnis abestō."

Wiser heads in Pentheus' family and among the populace try to dissuade him from this dangerous impiety. But rational advice only makes the young man more irrational and furious.

Hunc avus, hunc Athamās, hunc cētera turba suōrum
corripiunt dictīs frūstrāque inhibēre labōrant;
ācrior admonitū est inrītāturque retenta
et crēscit rabiēs, moderāminaque ipsa nocēbant:
sīc ego torrentem, quā nīl obstābat euntī,
lēnius et modicō strepitū dēcurrere vīdī;
at quācumque trabēs obstructaque saxa tenēbant,
spūmeus et fervēns et ab ōbice saevior ībat.

1. **What would be so preferable about a military conquest of Thebes?** (551–552)
2. **What would be so disgraceful about Bacchus' "conquest"?** (553)
3. **What disgusts Pentheus about Bacchus' interests and way of dressing? How does Ovid assign Pentheus prejudices that exist today, too?** (554–556)
4. **What does Pentheus intend to do with this hated "boy"?** (557–558)
5. **How does Acrisius serve as a noble model for Pentheus?** (559–560)
6. **What orders does Pentheus give?** (562–563)
7. **Who disagrees with Pentheus? What do they do?** (564–565)
8. **How successful are these people in impressing Pentheus?** (566–567)
9. **What is the basis of the comparison that Ovid now introduces? How does he work it out?** (568–571)
10. **How are we to feel about a man who resembles a torrential river?**

572 **Ecce**: now we learn the result of the savage commands of lines 562–563.
cruentō (1), to make bloody. The perfect passive participle means "bloodstained."
574 **comitem**: Ovid does not imply, as other narrators do, that this companion (Acoetes) is actually Bacchus in disguise. Acoetes, however, does tell a story that serves as a final warning to Pentheus.
575 **ligō** (1), to tie, bind.
576 **Tyrrhēnus, -a, um**, Tyrrhenian Greek, i.e., from Asia Minor. The Tyrrhenian Greeks migrated to Etruria in Italy, and the adjective **Tyrrhēnus** then came to mean Etruscan. Acoetes makes his origins quite clear in line 583.
577 **tremendus, -a, -um**, dreadful, terrible.
578 **poenae . . . tempora differt**: Ovid introduces a note of suspense by remarking on the postponement of punishment. The suspense continues to the end of Acoetes' long tale (691).
579 **documentum, -ī** (*n*), evidence.
581 **mōris . . . novī**: genitive of description.
cūr: introducing an indirect question after **ēde** (580).

582 **Ille**: Acoetes now briefly answers Pentheus' first questions (though he does not name his parents); then he responds to the last at length.
583 **Maeonia, -ae** (*f*), a region of Lydia, on the coast of Asia Minor.
584 **quae**: the "antecedent," **arva**, comes later in the line.
colerent: subjunctive in a relative clause of purpose.
arva . . . gregēs (585) . . . **armenta**: all objects of **relīquit**.
586 **pauper, pauperis** (*m*), impoverished man, poor man.
līnum, -ī (*n*), flax, thread, fishing line.
hāmus, -ī (*m*), hook, fishhook.
587 **calamus, -ī** (*m*), reed, fishing rod.
piscis, piscis (*m*), fish. Acoetes' father was a humble fisherman.
588 **illī**: dative of possession.
cēnsus, -ūs (*m*), census, wealth.
589 **quās**: the "antecedent" is **opēs** in line 590.
successor, successōris (*m*), successor, heir.
hērēs, hērēdis (*m*), heir.
591 **paternus, -a, -um**, of a father, paternal.

IV. *Tyrant versus Worshiper*

When Pentheus' servants return bloodied and beaten from their efforts to seize Bacchus, they only bring a simple follower of the god. On him the king vents his fury with a series of menacing questions.

Ecce cruentātī redeunt et, Bacchus ubi esset,
quaerentī dominō Bacchum vīdisse negārunt;
"Hunc," dīxēre, "tamen comitem famulumque sacrōrum
cēpimus," et trādunt manibus post terga ligātīs
sacra deī quondam Tyrrhēnā gente secūtum.
Adspicit hunc Pentheus oculīs, quōs īra tremendōs
fēcerat et, quamquam poenae vix tempora differt,
"Ō peritūre tuāque aliīs documenta datūre
morte," ait, "ēde tuum nōmen nōmenque parentum
et patriam mōrisque novī cūr sacra frequentēs."

This man, Acoetes, identifies himself as the son of a poor fisherman of Asia Minor. Brought up in poverty, he was left with nothing at his father's death.

Ille metū vacuus, "Nōmen mihi," dīxit, "Acoetēs,
patria Maeonia est, humilī dē plēbe parentēs.
Nōn mihi quae dūrī colerent pater arva iuvencī
lānigerōsve gregēs, nōn ūlla armenta relīquit;
pauper et ipse fuit līnōque solēbat et hāmīs
dēcipere et calamō salientēs dūcere piscēs.
Ars illī sua cēnsus erat; cum trāderet artem,
'Accipe, quās habeō, studiī successor et hērēs,'
dīxit, 'opēs,' moriēnsque mihī nihil ille relīquit
praeter aquās; ūnum hoc possum appellāre paternum.

1. **How well did Pentheus' servants carry out his orders? Was their task easy?** (572–573)
2. **Whom did they bring back with them and in what condition?** (574–576)
3. **What are Pentheus' feelings as he looks at the stranger?** (577–578)
4. **How do Pentheus' first words to the man alienate us?** (579–580)
5. **What is Acoetes' manner toward the menacing Pentheus? Are we on his side?** (582)
6. **What details about Acoetes' background contrast sharply with Pentheus' own circumstances and further incline us to his support?** (583–587)
7. **What did Acoetes' father have instead of property?** (588)
8. **Why do Acoetes and his father show no embarrassment about his occupation? What positive aspects of his work do the verbs in this section suggest?**
9. **What did Acoetes' father believe was the inheritance that he would leave his son? What does Acoetes himself call his inheritance?** (588–591)

592 **nē scopulīs haerērem**: Acoetes rebels against the career of fisherman.
593 **addiscō, addiscere** (3), **addidicī**, to learn further. The details that follow add up to the skills of a ship captain.
regimen, regiminis (*n*), guidance, (here) rudder.
moderor, moderārī (1), **moderātus sum**, to control, steer.
594 **Ōlenius, -a, -um**, of or belonging to Olenos in Aetolia or its founder of the same name. Olenos' daughter Aege was changed into a goat.
pluviālis, -is, -e, rainy.
Capella, -ae (*f*), the She Goat. The Olenian goat later became a star in the constellation Auriga, whose appearance coincided with much rain. Acoetes, like other ancient helmsmen, steers and plans his voyages by the stars.
595 **Tāygetē, -ēs** (*f*) (**-ēn** *Greek acc.*), daughter of Atlas and one of the Pleiades, a group of seven stars.
Hyadēs, -um (*f pl*), sisters of Hyas. The Hyades are a group of five stars whose rising and setting were associated with rainy weather.
Arctos, -ī (*f*) (**-on** *Greek acc.*), the Big Bear (also known to us as the Big Dipper).
596 **portus, -ūs** (*m*), port.
597 **forte**, by chance. A favorite introductory narrative particle for Ovid.
Dēlos, -ī (*f*), an island in the central Aegean.
Chīus, -a, -um, of Chios, an island near the coast of Asia Minor from which Acoetes has sailed.
598 **adplicō** (1), to steer to or toward. The passive form makes the verb intransitive and active in sense.
lītora: accusative of place to which, with the prepositional prefix **ad-** included in the verbs.
599 **saltus, -ūs** (*m*), jump, leap.
ūdus, -a, -um, damp, wet.
inmittō, inmittere (3), **inmīsī, inmissum**, to send to or on. **inmittor**: "I land on."
600 **Nox ubi cōnsumpta est**: after landing, Acoetes and the crew of course did many things, such as make a meal and bed down. Ovid jumps over all that and now quickly resumes the narrative with the next morning.
cōnsūmō, cōnsūmere (3), **cōnsumpsī, cōnsumptum**, to finish, consume.
Aurōra, -ae (*f*): Aurora, goddess of dawn, (here) daybreak.
rubēscō, rubēscere (3), **rubuī**, to grow red, blush.
prīmō (*adv.*), first, at first.
601 **exsurgō, exsurgere** (3), **exsurrēxī**, to rise, get up.
latex, laticis (*m*), liquid, water (for the trip).
recēns, recentis, recent, fresh.
602 **dūcat**: why subjunctive? **undās**: i.e., the spring from which the sailors are to fetch fresh water.
603 **tumulus, -ī** (*m*), mound, hill. **tumulō**: with **altō**.
prōmittat: subjunctive in an indirect question.

606 **nancīscor, nancīscī** (3), **nactus sum**, to find, get by chance.
607 **virgineus, -a, -um**, maidenly. **virgineā . . . fōrmā**: ablative of description defining the boy's girlish look.
608 **merum, -ī** (*n*), pure wine.
titubō (1), to stagger. From the start, there are indications that this "boy" is Bacchus.
609 **cultus, -ūs** (*m*), culture, style of clothes.
610 **posset**: subjunctive in a relative clause of characteristic.
611 **Quod**: interrogative adjective introducing an indirect question, "What . . . ?" Acoetes alone recognizes divinity.
612 **corpore sit . . . corpore . . . est**: note the skillful repetition in the second clause, and the significant change from subjunctive to indicative.
613 **faveās . . . adsīs**: Acoetes is praying to the boy whom he believes (correctly) to be a god.
614 **hīs**: Acoetes points to Opheltes and his shipmates.
venia, -ae (*f*), pardon.

V. *Acoetes Becomes a Navigator*

Acoetes decides to better his lot by learning navigation and becoming a ship captain. As captain on one voyage Acoetes steered his ship to Chios, landed, and spent the night ashore.

"Mox ego, nē scopulīs haererērem semper in īsdem,
addidicī regimen dextrā moderante carīnae
flectere et Ōleniae sīdus pluviāle Capellae
Tāygetēnque Hyadāsque oculīs Arctonque notāvī
ventōrumque domōs et portūs puppibus aptōs.
Forte petēns Dēlon Chīae tellūris ad ōrās
adplicor et dextrīs addūcor lītora rēmīs
dōque levēs saltūs ūdaeque inmittor harēnae.
Nox ubi cōnsumpta est (Aurōra rubēscere prīmō
coeperat), exsurgō laticēsque īnferre recentēs
admoneō mōnstrōque viam, quae dūcat ad undās.
Ipse quid aura mihī tumulō prōmittat ab altō
prōspiciō comitēsque vocō repetōque carīnam.

When the crew boarded the next day, they tried to drag along a young boy, intending to kidnap him and sell him later. Acoetes immediately observed the strange appearance and behavior of the child and suspected that he was in fact a god. So he prayed to him for favor and mercy.

"'Adsumus ēn!' inquit sociōrum prīmus Opheltēs,
utque putat, praedam dēsertō nactus in agrō
virgineā puerum dūcit per lītora fōrmā.
Ille merō somnōque gravis titubāre vidētur
vixque sequī; spectō cultum faciemque gradumque:
nīl ibi, quod crēdī posset mortāle, vidēbam.
Et sēnsī et dīxī sociīs: 'Quod nūmen in istō
corpore sit, dubitō, sed corpore nūmen in istō est.
Quisquis es, ō faveās nostrīsque labōribus adsīs.
hīs quoque dēs veniam.'

1. **Why did Acoetes decide to learn how to pilot a ship?** (592–593)
2. **What skills were involved?** (593–596)
3. **How does the ship approach Chios?** (597–598)
4. **What does Acoetes do when the ship touches sand?** (599)
5. **What task is assigned to the crew in the morning?** (600–602)
6. **What does Acoetes do at that same time?** (603–604)
7. **What kind of extra burden does the crew bring along when Acoetes recalls them? What is the sailors' purpose?** (605–607)
8. **What features of the boy does Acoetes notice, and what does he conclude from them?** (608–612)
9. **Can you fill out some of Ovid's brief details in lines 607–610 and describe more adequately this child and the special impression he makes?**
10. **How do Acoetes' words serve both as a warning to his companions and as a declaration of his simple piety?** (611–614)

614 **mitte**: "stop" (for **omitte**).
615 **quō**: ablative of comparison with **ōcior** (616).
cōnscendō, cōnscendere (3), **cōnscendī, cōnscēnsum**, to climb. **cōnscendere**: the infinitive depends on **ōcior**. Supply **erat** with **ōcior**.
616 **ōcior, ōciōris**, swifter, quicker.
antemna, -ae (*f*), sailyard.
prēnsō: perfect passive participle from **pre(he)ndere**.
rudēns, rudentis (*m*), rope.
relābor, relābī (3), **relāpsus sum**, to slide down or back.
617 **tutēla, -ae** (*f*), protection. The noun serves by metonymy to define Melanthus' role in watching for rocks and shallows, so that the prow might not drive on to them.
Melanthus: since the Greek word means "black," Ovid is playful in calling the sailor "blonde."
618 **quī . . . rēmīs** (619): Ovid describes the duties of the man who sets time for the rowers (in movies about Roman galleys often shown with a drum).
619 **Epōpeus**: the Greek word means "overseer."
620 **hōc omnēs**: supply **probant** from line 618. **hōc**: note that the neuter nominative and accusative singular sometimes have a long vowel for the sake of meter.
621 **sacrō . . . pondere**: Acoetes continues to regard the boy as a god, whose "sacred weight" would "violate" (and hence endanger) the ship.
pīnus, -ūs (*f*), pine, pinewood, (hence) a ship made from that timber.
622 **perpetior, perpetī** (3), **perpessus sum**, to permit.
pars . . . iūris: "I am in command here."
623 **obsistō**: Acoetes tries to block those who are dragging the boy aboard.
624 **Lycabās**: he seems modeled on Vergil's Mezentius, who also was exiled from his Etruscan city, and also was savage and violently scorned the gods.
625 **lūō, luere** (3), **luī**, to pay a penalty, suffer punishment.

626 **restō, restāre** (1), **restitī**, to withstand, oppose.
guttur, gutturis (*n*), throat (here, poetic plural).
pugnus, -ī (*m*), fist.
627 **rūpit**: lit., "broke," but since Acoetes lived to tell of his injury, we might use our colloquial "smashed."
excutiō, excutere (3), **excussī, excussum**, to drive or shake off (out of the way, overboard).
628 **āmēns**: not "crazy," but almost "unconscious" (from the blow).
retentus: lit., "held back," because Acoetes is holding on to the rope.
629 **factum**: Lycabas' violent assault on his captain. As before at lines 617–620, the crew's approval of impiety marks them all for punishment.
630 **clāmor, clāmōris** (*m*), shouting, noise.
631 **sopor, sopōris** (*m*), sleep, stupor. Cf. line 608.
āque: = **ā** + **-que** = **et ā merō**.
632 **Quā**: interrogative adjective, with **ope** (633).
634 **Prōreus**: with **dīxit** (635).
quōs . . . velīs (635): indirect question depending on **ēde**.
635 **ēde**: cf. line 580.
sistēre: 2nd person singular, future passive. That the boy will be landed where he asks is a false promise; but, as we shall see, the trusting Acoetes believes it.
636 **Naxos, -ī** (*f*), an Aegean island. **Naxon**: accusative of place to which (without a preposition for an island).
637 **hospitus, -a, -um**, hospitable.

VI. *Pious Acoetes versus Impious Crew*

Although the entire crew sneers at the possibility that the child might be a deity, Acoetes tries to prevent his coming aboard. This arouses the fury of the sailor Lycabas.

" 'Prō nōbīs mitte precārī,'
Dictys ait, quō nōn alius cōnscendere summās
ōcior antemnās prēnsōque rudente relābī;
hoc Libys, hoc flāvus, prōrae tutēla, Melanthus,
hoc probat Alcimedōn et, quī requiemque modumque
vōce dabat rēmīs, animōrum hortātor, Epōpeus,
hōc omnēs aliī: praedae tam caeca cupīdō est.
'Nōn tamen hanc sacrō violārī pondere pīnum
perpetiar,' dīxī; 'pars hīc mihi maximus iūris,'
inque aditū obsistō. Furit audacissimus omnī
dē numerō Lycabās, quī Tuscus pulsus ab urbe
exilium dīrā poenam prō caede luēbat.

Acting on his fury, Lycabas strikes Acoetes and nearly knocks him overboard. At this point, the child (whom Acoetes now confidently calls Bacchus) rouses himself and innocently asks for help. Assured that he will be landed at his desired destination, he requests to be taken to the island of Naxos.

"Is mihi, dum restō, iuvenālī guttura pugnō
rūpit et excussum mīsisset in aequora, sī nōn
haesissem quamvīs āmēns in fūne retentus.
Impia turba probat factum; tum dēnique Bacchus
(Bacchus enim fuerat), velutī clāmōre solūtus
sit sopor āque merō redeant in pectora sēnsūs,
'Quid facitis? Quis clāmor?' ait. 'Quā, dīcite, nautae,
hūc ope pervēnī? Quō mē dēferre parātis?'
'Pōne metum,' Prōreus, 'et quōs contingere portūs
ēde velīs,' dīxit: 'terrā sistēre petītā.'
'Naxon,' ait Līber, 'cursūs advertite vestrōs.
Illa mihī domus est, vōbīs erit hospita tellūs.'

1. **What is the immediate response of the crew to Acoetes' prayer? How far would Pentheus have agreed with them?** (614–615)
2. **How does Ovid individualize some of the crew here?** (615–619)
3. **Instead of piety, what motivates the sailors?** (620)
4. **What good reasons does Acoetes give for opposing the crew? What does he do?** (621–623)
5. **What facts about Lycabas' past make him an appropriate mutineer?** (623–625)
6. **What does he do to Acoetes?** (626–628)
7. **How do the rest feel at this violent treatment of their captain? What key adjective defines them?** (629)
8. **Although the captain has failed to move them, the sailors are given a second chance to escape punishment by Bacchus. What does the boy-god do?** (630–633)
9. **How does Proreus quiet the boy's anxiety?** (634–635)
10. **What does the boy offer the crew for taking him to his destination?** (636–637)

638 **fallācēs**: in falsely swearing to a god, the sailors utterly doom themselves.
639 **fore**: future infinitive in indirect statement. Supply as subject **id**, i.e., the sworn promise.
pictae . . . carīnae: "ship brightly painted."
640 **Dextera . . . dextrā**: note the clever variation.
dextrā: "on the right," "to the right."
linteum, -ī (*n*), linen cloth, (here) sail.
641 **dēmēns . . . furor**: the impious crew invert the sense of these words, as they use for the pious simplicity of Acoetes what properly applies to their own actions.
642 **timet**: the sailors apparently fear punishment if they deliver the boy to his destination.
nūtū: instrumental ablative, "by a nod of the head."
643 **aure**: supply **in**.
susurrō (1), to whisper.
644 **moderāmen, moderāminis** (*n*), management, (here) rudder.
645 **ministerium, -ī** (*n*), function, performance. **ministeriō**: ablative of separation.
scelerisque artisque: when two nouns of different senses depend on the same word (noun or verb), the rhetorical effect is called *zeugma* (from the Greek word for "yoke"). Thus here Acoetes removed himself from the *perpetration* of a crime and also from the *practice* of the art of shipmaster. The two italicized words render the separate aspects of **ministeriō** implied by **sceleris** and **artis**.
646 **inmurmurō** (1), to mutter against or into.
647 **Tē . . . in ūnō**: "In you alone."
649 **expleō, explēre** (2), **explēvī, explētum**, to fill, fulfil.
Naxō . . . relictā: ablative absolute.
dīversa: supply **loca**.

650 **inlūdō, inlūdere** (3), **inlūsī, inlūsum**, to play, fool. Bacchus has recognized the sailors' impiety and dishonesty all the time, but he plays with their efforts to be brutal kidnappers.
modo dēnique: "only now at last."
651 **puppī pontum prōspectat**: the multiple alliteration of *p* may reinforce the note of play-acting on the part of Bacchus.
aduncus, -a, -um, hooked, curved.
652 ***flēō, flēre** (2), **flēvī, flētum**, to cry, weep.
flentī: dative of the present participle, with **similis**.
653 **prōmīsistis**: the god refers to the promise made in line 635.
655 **puerum iuvenēs . . . multī . . . ūnum**: the disposition of the nouns and their adjectives is *chiastic* (ABBA).
656 **flēbam**: Acoetes, who pities the god and does not know that he has complete mastery of the situation, is indeed rather ridiculous in his simplemindedness.
657 **inpellō, inpellere** (3), **inpulsī, inpulsum**, to strike on, strike against.

VII. *Vain Attempts to Deceive the God*

When Acoetes takes the crew's promises at face value and starts to steer for Naxos, they all angrily assail his simple honesty. He therefore abandons his command, since it can only result, he realizes, in impiety.

"Per mare fallācēs perque omnia nūmina iūrant
sīc fore mēque iubent pictae dare vēla carīnae.
Dextera Naxos erat: dextrā mihi lintea dantī
'Quid facis, ō dēmēns? Quis tē furor,' inquit, 'Acoete?'
Prō sē quisque timet: 'Laevam pete,' maxima nūtū
pars mihi significat, pars, quid velit, aure susurrat.
Obstipuī, 'Capiat'que 'aliquis moderāmina,' dīxī,
mēque ministeriō scelerisque artisque remōvī.
Increpor ā cūnctīs, tōtumque inmurmurat agmen;
ē quibus Aethaliōn, 'Tē scīlicet omnis in ūnō
nostra salūs posita est,' ait et subit ipse meumque
explet opus Naxōque petit dīversa relictā.

Now the god begins to act, pretending to cry and complain against the unfulfilled promise: a final test and chance for the crew to correct their behavior. They, however, mock the god's tears and persist in making for a different port.

"Tum deus inlūdēns, tamquam modo dēnique fraudem
sēnserit, ē puppī pontum prōspectat aduncā
et flentī similis, 'Nōn haec mihi lītora, nautae,
prōmīsistis,' ait. 'Nōn haec mihi terra rogāta est.
Quō meruī poenam factō? Quae glōria vestra est,
sī puerum iuvenēs, sī multī fallitis ūnum?'
Iamdūdum flēbam: lacrimās manus impia nostrās
rīdet et inpellit properantibus aequora rēmīs.

1. **What is the crew's response to the boy's request to be taken to Naxos?** (638–639)
2. **What does Acoetes do then?** (640)
3. **What does the crew really want? How do they separately indicate their meaning to Acoetes?** (641–643)
4. **Why does Acoetes not agree to follow their urging?** (644–645)
5. **How essential is Acoetes' role on the ship?** (646–648)
6. **What does Acoetes' replacement do?** (648–649)
7. **In what respects was Bacchus play-acting when he appealed to the crew? What did Acoetes think at that time?** (650–656)
8. **How does the speech of Bacchus win our sympathy? How does Ovid use stage directions to incline our feelings?** (652–656)
9. **What difference does it make to our attitude whether a boy or a god made the speech?**
10. **How does the crew prove its impiety in its response?** (656–657)

658 **tibi**: with **adiūrō** (659).
ipsum: i.e., Bacchus.
praesēns, praesentis, present. A god's active presence is regularly assumed and dreaded as a sign of his divinity.
659 **tam**: with **vēra** and coordinate with **quam** in line 660.
mē . . . referre: indirect statement.
660 **vērī**: objective genitive, dependent on **fidē**.
fidē: ablative of comparison with **maiōra**.
vērī maiōra fidē: "too great to be believed true."
661 **siccum nāvāle**: "naval drydock."
663 **dēdūcunt**: "they unfurl."
664 **hedera, -ae** (*f*), ivy.
nexus, -ūs (*m*), knots, coil, entwining.
recurvus, -a, -um, curved back, winding.
665 **serpō, serpere** (3), **serpsī, serptum**, to creep, crawl.
gravidus, -a, -um, heavy, full, pregnant.
distinguō, distinguere (3), **distīnxī, distīnctum**, to distinguish, decorate.
corymbus, -ī (*m*), cluster (of ivy berries).
666 **Ipse**: i.e., Bacchus.
racēmifer, racēmifera, racēmiferum, cluster-bearing, clustering. Ovid has invented this word, to sound "epic."
667 **pampineus, -a, -um**, full of vine leaves.
668 **quem**: i.e., Bacchus.
lynx, lyncis (*m/f*), lynx. These wild animals, like the ivy and grape vines, were constant associates of Bacchic rites.
669 **panthēra, -ae** (*f*), panther. Note the rare double spondee that this produces at the line end.

670 **hōc**: neuter accusative singular.
672 **expressō . . . curvāmine**: "when the spine was forced into a curve."
673 **incipit**: supply **dīcere**.
674 **rictus, -ūs** (*m*), open mouth.
pandus, -a, -um, snubbed (of nose).
675 **nāris, nāris** (*f*), nostril.
squāma, -ae (*f*), scales, scaly skin.
dūrō (1), to harden. Ovid has now described the transformation of two crewmen into dolphins by concentrating on individual details.
676 **obvertō, obvertere** (3), **obvertī, obversum**, to turn toward.
677 **manūs**: Ovid offers a new detail of metamorphosis: hands into dolphin fins or flippers.
678 **pinna, -ae** (*f*), feather, wing, (of fish) fin.

VIII. *The Epiphany of Bacchus*

The god asserts himself, stopping the moving ship dead in the sea, wreathing it with ivy and grapevines, and filling it with seemingly dangerous wild beasts.

"Per tibi nunc ipsum (nec enim praesentior illō
est deus) adiūrō, tam mē tibi vēra referre
quam vērī maiōra fidē: stetit aequore puppis
haud aliter, quam sī siccum nāvāle tenēret.
Illī admīrantēs rēmōrum in verbere perstant
vēlaque dēdūcunt gemināque ope currere temptant.
Inpediunt hederae rēmōs nexūque recurvō
serpunt et gravidīs distingunt vēla corymbīs.
Ipse racēmiferīs frontem circumdatus ūvīs
pampineīs agitat vēlātam frondibus hastam;
quem circā tigrēs simulacraque inānia lyncum
pictārumque iacent fera corpora panthērārum.

In panic, the crew rise up. One member of the crew leaps overboard and is turned into a dolphin. Two others, while they wildly respond to the crisis, suffer similar metamorphoses.

"Exsiluēre virī, sīve hōc īnsānia fēcit
sīve timor, prīmusque Medōn nigrēscere coepit
corpore et expressō spīnae curvāmine flectī.
Incipit huic Lycabās: 'In quae mīrācula,' dīxit,
'verteris?' et lātī rictūs et panda loquentī
nāris erat squāmamque cutis dūrāta trahēbat.
At Libys obstantēs dum vult obvertere rēmōs,
in spatium resilīre manūs breve vīdit et illās
iam nōn esse manūs, iam pinnās posse vocārī.

1. **What features of Acoetes' oath in lines 658–660 would probably irritate Pentheus?**
2. **Why does Acoetes insist on both the truth and incredibility of his facts?** (659–660)
3. **What miracle occurs to the ship?** (660–661)
4. **Although the sailors are surprised, how do they try to counteract this marvel?** (662–663)
5. **What happens to the oars and sails?** (664–665)
6. **How does the boy now manifest himself as a god?** (666–669)
7. **What alternative causes account for the wild reactions of the crew?** (670–671)
8. **How complete a description of a dolphin is produced by the details of Medon's change?** (671–672)
9. **What supplementary features emerge when we turn to Lycabas? How appropriately do they begin?** (674–675)
10. **How does the transformation of Libys also start aptly and add to the total dolphin description?** (676–678)

679 **intortus, -a, -um**, twisted.
680 **truncus, -a, -um**, mutilated, deprived of limbs.
truncō: with **corpore** (681).
repandus, -a, -um, with snout turned back (cf. line 674).
681 **falcātus, -a, -um**, sickle-shaped, curved.
novissimus, -a, -um, very new, recent (since it has just become a tail).
cauda, -ae (*f*), tail. Ovid has now accounted for changes in the lower body, to fill out the picture of the dolphin.
682 **cornua lūnae**: what is the effect of this comparison of the crescent moon to a dolphin's tail?
683 **dant saltūs**: leaping dolphins are a familiar phenomenon.
adspergō, adsperginis (*f*), spray.
rōrant: "they are sprinkled," "they are soaked."
684 **ēmergō, ēmergere** (3), **ēmersī, ēmersum**, to emerge, rise out.
685 **lascīvus, -a, -um**, playful.
686 **patulus, -a, -um**, wide open.
687 **Dē modo vīgintī**: "Of recently twenty (men)."
688 **pavidus, -a, -um**, trembling, fearful. Supply **mē**.
689 **vix . . . meum**: "hardly myself."
690 **Dīa, -ae** (*f*): Dia is the old name for Naxos, where Bacchus had wanted to land (cf. line 636).
Dēlātus: cf. **dēferre** (633).
691 **Bacchēus, -a, -um**, of Bacchus.
sacra frequentō: Acoetes thus brings to an end his long reply by echoing the final words of Pentheus' question in line 581, **sacra frequentēs**.

692 **ambāgēs, ambāgum** (*f pl*), roundabout way, digression, long-winded speech.
693 **absūmō, absūmere** (3), **absumpsī, absumptum**, to diminish, destroy.
694 **famulī, rapite**: Pentheus rashly orders his slaves to brutal acts, as he had vainly done before in lines 562–563.
cruciō (1), to crucify, torture.
695 **corpora**: poetic plural.
696 **solidīs . . . tēctīs** (697): "strongly built prison."
698 **īnstrūmenta**: predicate noun.
ferrumque: subject with **ignēsque**.
699 **patuisse**: infinitive in indirect statement depending on **fāma est** (700).
lāpsās: supply **esse**; its subject is **catēnās** (700).
700 **nūllō solvente**: ablative absolute.

IX. *Pentheus Misses the Story's Point*

When the entire crew of nineteen has been transformed, Acoetes alone, with the blessing of Bacchus, steers the ship to the rightful port of Naxos. Ever since, he concludes his account, he has been a fervent devotee of Bacchus.

"Alter ad intortōs cupiēns dare bracchia fūnēs
bracchia nōn habuit truncōque repandus in undās
corpore dēsiluit: falcāta novissima cauda est,
quālia dīmidiae sinuantur cornua lūnae.
Undique dant saltūs multāque adspergine rōrant
ēmerguntque iterum redeuntque sub aequora rūrsus
inque chorī lūdunt speciem lascīvaque iactant
corpora et acceptum patulīs mare nāribus efflant.
Dē modo vīgintī (tot enim ratis illa ferēbat)
restābam sōlus: pavidum gelidumque trementī
corpore vixque meum firmat deus, 'Excute,' dīcēns,
'corde metum Dīamque tenē.' Dēlātus in illam
accessī sacrīs Bacchēaque sacra frequentō."

Unimpressed by this pious story, indeed barely controlling his anger during its narration, Pentheus orders Acoetes to be tortured and then put to death. Miraculously, however, Acoetes escapes from chains and prison.

"Praebuimus longīs," Pentheus, "ambāgibus aurēs,"
inquit, "ut īra morā vīrēs absūmere posset.
Praecipitem, famulī, rapite hunc cruciātaque dīrīs
corpora tormentīs Stygiae dēmittite noctī."
Prōtinus abstractus solidīs Tyrrhēnus Acoetēs
clauditur in tēctīs; et dum crūdēlia iussae
īnstrūmenta necis ferrumque ignēsque parantur,
sponte suā patuisse forēs lāpsāsque lacertīs
sponte suā fāma est nūllō solvente catēnās.

1. **How does the transformation of another sailor complete the anatomical rendering of a dolphin?** (679–681)
2. **How is the simile effective in bringing the entire description of metamorphosis to a neat close?** (682)
3. **On the basis of the way Acoetes narrates the movements of the new fish, how are we to regard the acts of the god: cruel, just, or what?** (683–686)
4. **How has Acoetes himself reacted to the scene?** (688–689)
5. **What does Bacchus tell him to do now?** (689–690)
6. **What has been the effect of this whole experience on Acoetes?** (691)
7. **Acoetes' final words in line 691 indicate that he has been answering Pentheus' question in line 581. How does his answer also warn Pentheus?**
8. **If Pentheus had been able to listen to Acoetes' words, how might he have applied them profitably to his own situation?**
9. **Instead, what do Pentheus' first words show about his attention?** (692–693)
10. **How do Pentheus' actions now compare with those of the sailors?** (694–695)
11. **What happens to all the devices that are supposed to keep Acoetes securely in custody?** (696–700)

701 **Perstat**: the stubborn persistence of Pentheus in spite of all the warnings and miracles demands his ruin.

702 **ēlēctus, -a, -um**, chosen, selected.

Cithaerōn: a mountain near Thebes.

703 **bacchantēs, bacchantum** (*f pl*), female followers of Bacchus.

704 **bellicus, -a, -um**, involved in war, warlike. Modifies **tubicen** (705).

canōrus, -a, -um, tuneful, melodious.

705 **tubicen, tubicinis** (*m*), trumpeter.

706 **ictus, -a, -um**, struck.

707 **recandēscō, recandēscere** (3), **recanduī**, to grow white or hot again. As an angry tyrant, Pentheus loses all sympathy before his death.

708 **Monte ferē mediō**: "Almost in the middle of the mountain"; we are given a central focus for the scene of the final tragedy.

est: the subject is delayed to the last word of the next line, **campus**.

cingentibus . . . silvīs: ablative absolute. Otherwise densely wooded, Cithaeron has this one open field in its center.

ultima: accusative plural, the "limits" or "borders" of the **campus**.

709 **pūrus, -a, -um**, clean, clear, pure, free (from).

spectābilis, -is, -e, visible.

710 **illum**: i.e., Pentheus.

profānus, -a, -um, wicked, impious.

711 **videt . . . violāvit** (712): the subject is **māter** in line 713.

712 **suum . . . Penthea**: "her own (son) Pentheus."

713 **māter**: i.e., Agave (finally named in line 725).

714 **aper, aprī** (*m*), boar. Bacchus deludes the mother into the conviction that her son is a wild beast, fit for sacrifice to the god.

715 **feriendus**: supply **est**.

omnis in ūnum: dramatic contrast, which highlights the helpless isolation of Pentheus.

716 **trepidum . . . trepidum** (717) . . . **loquentem . . . damnantem** (718) . . . **fatentem**: the accusative adjectives and participles all refer to Pentheus.

717 **violentus, -a, -um**, violent. **verba minus violenta**: cf. such wild speeches as that of 692–695.

718 **peccāsse** (*syncopated form of the perfect active infinitive*): indirect statement following **fatentem**.

719 **mātertera, -ae** (*f*), mother's sister, aunt. Here in the vocative with the name in line 720.

720 **Autonoē, -ēs** (*f*), another daughter of Cadmus and mother of Pentheus' cousin Actaeon.

Actaeōn, Actaeonis (*m*): a Theban prince, he had died a tragic death, as told earlier by Ovid in the *Metamorphoses* (III.138–252). Having angered Diana by blundering near the pool where she was bathing, he was changed into a deer and torn apart by his own hunting dogs. In Ovid's poem the pool of Diana anticipates the fatal pool of Narcissus, and the manner of Actaeon's death (viewed as an animal, a god's victim) prefigures Pentheus' cruel end.

X. *Pentheus Spies on Forbidden Rites*

Pentheus cannot yield to any kind of warning. He decides to go and spy on the secret rites of Bacchus' followers. The scene for the tragic finale, an open field amid the woods of Mount Cithaeron, is set by Ovid.

Perstat Echīonidēs nec iam iubet īre, sed ipse
vādit, ubi ēlēctus facienda ad sacra Cithaerōn
cantibus et clārā bacchantum vōce sonābat.
Ut fremit ācer equus, cum bellicus aere canōrō
signa dedit tubicen, pugnaeque adsūmit amōrem,
Penthea sīc ictus longīs ululātibus aethēr
mōvit, et audītō clāmōre recanduit īra.
Monte ferē mediō est cingentibus ultima silvīs,
pūrus ab arboribus, spectābilis undique campus.

As he watches what outsiders are forbidden to observe, Pentheus is noticed and attacked by his mother and aunts, who perceive him as an alien being indeed: as an animal that should be sacrificed to Bacchus.

Hīc oculīs illum cernentem sacra profānīs
prīma videt, prīma est īnsānō concita cursū,
prīma suum missō violāvit Penthea thyrsō
māter et, "Ō geminae," clāmāvit, "adeste sorōrēs.
Ille aper, in nostrīs errat quī maximus agrīs,
ille mihi feriendus aper." Ruit omnis in ūnum
turba furēns: cūnctae coeunt trepidumque sequuntur
iam trepidum, iam verba minus violenta loquentem,
iam sē damnantem, iam sē peccāsse fatentem.
Saucius ille tamen, "Fer opem, mātertera," dīxit,
"Autonoē. Moveant animōs Actaeonis umbrae."

1. **Do you think that Pentheus still had a chance, after the miraculous escape of Acoetes, to change his attitude and save himself? What supports your conclusion?**
2. **In deciding to go to Cithaeron, how does Pentheus utterly doom himself? How does this fit well Tiresias' prediction in lines 517–518?** (702–703)
3. **Explain the comparison (simile) in lines 704–707. Why is it ironically appropriate to liken Pentheus to that special kind of horse?**
4. **How does the brief description of the field on the mountain give a clear focus to the events that follow?** (708–709)
5. **How is Pentheus' guilt summarized in line 710?**
6. **Who is the first to spot Pentheus? What action does she take? What does she think she sees?** (711–715)
7. **What then do she and the others do to Pentheus? How is this *turba furēns* a grotesque answer to Pentheus' earlier protest against Bacchic *furor (531)*?** (715–716)
8. **What does Pentheus do to save himself? How can we see the ironic working out of Tiresias' prophecy?** (716–718)
9. **How does Pentheus' appeal to Autonoe, Actaeon's mother, affect us? To what extent does Ovid allow us now to begin pitying Pentheus?** (719–720)

721 **dextram . . . precantis**: note the grotesque detail: Pentheus holds out his right hand in supplication, and his aunt, with divinely induced strength, wrenches it off. Ovid likes to record such "answers" to prayer.

722 **auferō, auferre** (*irreg.*), **abstulī, ablātum**, to take away.

Īnōus, -a, -um, of Ino, still another sister of Agave and hence another aunt of Pentheus.

lacerō (1), to tear apart. This fulfills the prophecy of Tiresias (cf. **lacer** in line 522).

723 **tendat**: why subjunctive?

724 **trunca . . . dēiectīs**: Pentheus resembles a tree whose branches and limbs have been lopped off.

725 **Vīsīs**: "at what she saw." Agave's bestial howl is not the maternal reaction Pentheus expected.

726 **iactō** (1), to toss, hurl. The motion of head and hair here indicates the wildness of Agave's state.

727 **āvellō, āvellere** (3), **āvulsī, āvulsum**, to pluck, tear off or away. **āvulsumque caput**: direct object of **conplexa**. With superhuman strength, Agave has torn her son's head off and now "lovingly" embraces it.

728 **iō** (*interjection*), ho! Agave's speech about "victory" shows just how unaware she is. In Euripides' Greek tragedy, she recovers her senses and discovers, to her horror, her son's head in her bloody hands.

729 **frondēs**: Ovid spells out in a final simile the implicit tree-image of line 724.

citō (*adv.*), quickly.

autumnus, -ī (*m*), autumn.

730 **arbore**: ablative of separation.

731 **nefandus, -a, -um**, unspeakable, impious.

732 **sacra frequentant**: Ovid here echoes lines 581 and 691.

733 **tūs, tūris** (*n*), incense.

Ismēnis, Ismēnidos, a woman of Thebes (the Ismenos being the city's river).

XI. *The Fatal Moment*

The prediction of Tiresias achieves total fulfillment: Pentheus is torn limb from limb, and his mother completes the kill by wrenching off his head. All of this confirms the Thebans in their worship of the powerful godhead of Bacchus.

Illa, quis Actaeōn, nescit dextramque precantis
abstulit, Īnōō lacerāta est altera raptū.
Nōn habet īnfēlīx, quae mātrī bracchia tendat,
trunca sed ostendēns dēiectīs vulnera membrīs,
"Adspice, māter," ait. Vīsīs ululāvit Agāvē
collaque iactāvit mōvitque per āera crīnem
āvulsumque caput digitīs conplexa cruentīs
clāmat, "Iō comitēs, opus hoc victōria nostra est."
Nōn citius frondēs autumnī frīgore tactās
iamque male haerentēs altā rapit arbore ventus,
quam sunt membra virī manibus dīrepta nefandīs.
Tālibus exemplīs monitae nova sacra frequentant
tūraque dant sanctāsque colunt Ismēnides ārās.

1. **What effect does the name of Actaeon have on Pentheus' aunt? Why? What effect does it have on us?** (721–722)
2. **What problem faces Pentheus as he tries to appeal to his mother by gesture and word? How does he handle it?** (723–725)
3. **How is Agave affected by the pathetic sight of her son? What do her actions indicate?** (725–727)
4. **What does she call her "victory"?** (728)
5. **What in your opinion is the effect of the simile in lines 729–730?**
6. **In what specific ways has Tiresias' prophecy in lines 519–525 been carried out?**
7. **Do you feel that Ovid has tried to make Bacchus out to be a cruel and mysterious deity? Or has he turned the myth into a human tragedy, where the person and activity of the god recede from attention? Support your answers with references to specific passages in the story.**

PASSAGES FOR COMPARISON

BAUCIS AND PHILEMON

Genesis 18 and 19

Issues similar to those in the story of Baucis and Philemon appear in two adjacent stories in Genesis: that of the Lord's appearance to Abraham and that of his angels' appearance to Lot, the only righteous inhabitant of Sodom. First, the angels and the Lord, disguised as men, come to Abraham, who hastens to welcome them, saying, ". . . do not pass by your servant. Let a little water be brought, and wash your feet, and rest yourselves under the tree, while I fetch a morsel of bread. . . ." Abraham then hurries to Sarah, his wife, and tells her to make quickly three cakes of "fine meal." He then commands the servant to prepare a calf, "tender and good," while he himself fetches curds and milk. When all is ready, he "set it before them; and he stood by them under the tree while they ate."

After the feast the Lord tells Abraham that Sarah will bear a child in the spring. Because of her and her husband's advanced age, Sarah laughs to herself in disbelief. In spite of her lack of faith, the Lord nevertheless not only reveals himself to Abraham but also tells him his plan to destroy the nearby city of Sodom for its wickedness. Abraham, apologizing for his boldness, persuades the Lord to spare Sodom if ten righteous persons are found in it.

When the angels of the Lord come to Sodom, Lot, who is sitting at the gate of the city, invites them home: "My lords, turn aside, I pray you, to your servant's house and spend the night, and wash your feet; then you may rise up early and go on your way." They return to his house, where he "made them a feast, and baked unleavened bread, and they ate." Afterwards, all the men of Sodom come to Lot's house and ask him to put his guests outside so that they may have homosexual relations with them. Lot refuses because a host's responsibility to his guests takes precedence over all other demands, and he offers his unmarried daughters instead. When these are refused and the men of Sodom still insist upon "knowing" the guests, the angels tell Lot they are going to rescue him and his wife and daughters from the city, advising him to "flee to the hills." They warn him, however, that no one may look back at the city. When Lot's wife does so, she becomes a pillar of salt, while the Lord destroys Sodom with "brimstone and fire." Its destruction is total: ". . . and lo, the smoke of the land went up like the smoke of a furnace." (*The New Oxford Annotated Bible, RSV.*)

ACIS, GALATEA, AND POLYPHEMUS

Selections from Homer's *Odyssey*, Book IX

The Greek poet Homer (eighth century B.C.) wrote two epics about the Trojan War (ca. 1250 B.C.?) and its heroes. The *Odyssey* describes the travels and homecoming of one hero, Odysseus, after the war is over. He visits many strange lands and survives harrowing adventures, including a sojourn on the island of the Cyclopes. In Book IX he tells the story of his encounter with Polyphemus, describing the giant and his cave (Richmond Lattimore, translator):

"Inside
there lodged a monster of a man, who now was herding
the flocks at a distance away, alone, for he did not range with
others, but stayed away by himself; his mind was lawless,
and in truth he was a monstrous wonder made to behold, not
like a man, an eater of bread, but more like a wooded
peak of the high mountains seen standing away from the others. . . .
We went inside the cave and admired everything inside it.
Baskets were there, heavy with cheeses, and the pens crowded
with lambs and kids. They had all been divided into separate
groups, the firstlings in one place, and then the middle ones,
the babies again by themselves. And all his vessels, milk pails
and pans, that he used for milking into, were running over
with whey."

Odysseus, using the name Nobody, asks Polyphemus for hospitality, but instead arouses the giant's hostility.

" 'We are your suppliants,
and Zeus the guest god, who stands behind all strangers with honors
due them, avenges any wrong toward strangers and suppliants.'
So I spoke, but he answered me in pitiless spirit:
'Stranger, you are a simple fool, or come from far off,
when you tell me to avoid the wrath of the gods or fear them.
The Cyclopes do not concern themselves over Zeus of the aegis,
nor any of the rest of the blessed gods, since we are far better
than they, and for fear of the hate of Zeus I would not spare
you or your companions either, if the fancy took me
otherwise. . . .'
[He] sprang up and reached for my companions,
caught up two together and slapped them, like killing puppies,
against the ground, and the brains ran all over the floor, soaking
the ground. Then he cut them up limb by limb and got supper ready,
and like a lion reared in the hills, without leaving anything,
ate them, entrails, flesh and the marrowy bones alike."

Polyphemus imprisons Odysseus and his men with him in the cave. The next day, having made the Cyclops drunk with wine, the companions blind the giant as he sleeps. They ride past him out of the cave, clinging to the undersides of Polyphemus' sheep as he feels their backs for riders.

"Last of all the flock the ram went out of the doorway,
loaded with his own fleece, and with me, and my close counsels.
Then, feeling him, powerful Polyphemos spoke a word to him:
'My dear old ram, why are you thus leaving the cave last of
the sheep? Never in the old days were you left behind by
the flock, but long-striding, far ahead of the rest would pasture
on the tender bloom of the grass, be first at running rivers,
and be eager always to lead the way first back to the sheepfold
at evening. Now you are last of all. Perhaps you are grieving
for your master's eye, which a bad man with his wicked companions
put out, after he had made my brain helpless with wine, this
Nobody, who I think has not yet got clear of destruction.' "

From the ship, Odysseus taunts the blind giant and reveals his true name.

"So I spoke, and still more the heart in him was angered.
He broke away the peak of a great mountain and let it
fly, and threw it in front of the dark-prowed ship by only
a little, it just failed to graze the steering oar's edge. . . .
He groaned aloud and answered me, saying:
'Ah now, a prophecy spoken of old is come to completion.
There used to be a man here, great and strong, and a prophet
Telemos, Eurymos' son, who for prophecy was pre-eminent
and grew old as a prophet among the Cyclopes. This man told me
how all this that has happened now must someday be accomplished,
and how I must lose the sight of my eye at the hands of Odysseus.' "

Theocritus' *Idyll* XI

Theocritus (ca. 300–ca. 260 B.C.?) was a Sicilian Greek who probably spent his adult life in Alexandria, the literary capital of the age. In contrast with Homer, he wrote short poems (the *Idylls*), usually about love and often set in a rural or "pastoral" landscape. His witty achievement in *Idyll* XI is to make Homer's repulsive giant into an attractive lover. The poet begins by saying that there is "no other cure for love . . . only the Muses," that is, poetry. His proof is Polyphemus (Anthony Holden, translator):

It's how the Cyclops my countryman found comfort
in his love for Galatea. Polyphemus, so the old story goes,
the beard still fresh around his lips and temples,
loved her not with apples, with roses or locks of hair,
but with headlong passion. All else seemed worthless.
Often his sheep would return of their own accord
from their green pastures to the fold, as he sat
on the shore, amid the seaweed, wasting away
with love, singing all day of Galatea. . . .
"Pale Galatea, paler than cream,
why cast your love away?
Gentler than lamb, livelier
than calf, ripe as reddening grape,
why come to me only in my sweet sleep?
I've loved you, lady, since first you came
with your mother to pick hyacinths on my hill.
I showed you the way. And since that hour,
since I saw you, my love has not changed.
But you, by Zeus, you think nothing of me.
Yet I know, pretty one, why you run away.
It's because of my eyebrow, my single eyebrow,
which stretches across the full width of my face,
from ear to ear, one, long and hairy;
and because of the single eye beneath it,
and the one broad nostril above my lip.
Such I am. Yet still I herd a thousand cattle,
and the milk I drink is theirs, the richest.
Never am I without cheese, summer or autumn,
or deepest winter; my kegs are always full.
And I can sing as no other Cyclops—
often of you, sweet apple of my love,
and of myself, I sing deep into the night.
For you I am raising eleven fawns, each

with a collar, and four bear cubs.
Come to me; come, and you'll never lack a thing. . . .
But if you think me too rough, too ragged,
I've logs of oak, an undying fire,
beneath those ashes; I offer you my soul
to burn, and my single eye as well,
than which, believe me, I love nothing more. . . ."

In spite of his passion, by the poem's end Polyphemus has persuaded himself that he'll one day "find another Galatea, another more fair." The poet concludes,

So Polyphemus shepherded his love with song
and found more comfort than money could buy.

NARCISSUS AND ECHO

The Pool of Diana

Earlier in Book III, Ovid creates in the pool of Diana a prototype for the disastrous pool that helps to bring about Narcissus' ruin. As the goddess bathes in her special forest pool, the Theban prince Actaeon innocently blunders into the spot and accidentally sees the nude deity. He is not allowed to escape alive but is transformed into a deer and killed by his own hunting dogs. This excerpt (M. Innes, translator) gives lines 155–181 of Book III:

> There was a valley, thickly overgrown with pitchpine and with sharp-needled cypress trees. It was called Gargaphie and was sacred to Diana, the goddess of the hunt. Far in its depths lay a woodland cave, which no hand of man had wrought: but nature by her own devices had imitated art. She had carved a natural arch from the living stone and the soft tufa rocks. On the right hand was a murmuring spring of clear water, spreading out into a wide pool with grassy banks. Here the goddess, when she was tired with hunting in the woods, used to bathe her virginal limbs in the pure water. . . .
>
> While Diana was bathing there in her usual stream, Actaeon, who had for the present abandoned his hunting, came wandering with hesitant steps through the woods which he had never seen before. He reached the grove—so were the fates directing him—and entered the cave, which was moist with spray. The nymphs, discovered in their nakedness, beat their breasts at the sight of a man, and filled all the grove with their sudden outcry. Crowding around Diana, they shielded her with their own bodies.

The Narcissus of Guillaume de Lorris

The important allegorical poem, *The Romance of the Rose,* was composed in the thirteenth century under the influence of the Ovidian Revival. The first portion of the poem, completed by Guillaume de Lorris before his death in 1235, includes a retelling of the tale of Narcissus, with a moral for the ladies: not to reject their lovers, for fear of God's punishment. The tale of Ovid, as can be quickly seen, is considerably simplified: Echo is just a "fine lady" who pines away for love of Narcissus and, dying, curses him. There is no reference to metamorphosis of either her or the boy (Harry W. Robbins, translator):

Narcissus was a youth whom Love once caught
Within his snare and caused such dole and woe
That in his grief he rendered up his ghost.
Now Echo, a fine lady, loved him more

Than any creature born, and was for him
So lovesick that she said she needs must die
If she had not his love. But of his own
Beauty he was so proud that hers he scorned,
And neither for her weeping nor her prayers
Would satisfy her passion. When she knew
Herself refused, she suffered so much pain
And anger, and she took it in such despite,
That hopelessly she pined away and died.
But just before the end she prayed to God,
And this was her request: that whom she found
Disloyal to her love, Narcissus' self
In his hard heart should someday tortured be
And burn with such a love that he would find
No joy in any thing; thus he might know
And comprehend what woe a loyal maid
Had felt when she so vilely was refused.
The prayer was reasonable, and therefore God
Ordained that she this recompense should have;
And so Narcissus, as one day by chance,
Returning from the hunt, tired with the chase
That up and down the hills had led him far,
He came upon that fountain clear and pure,
Beneath the shadow of the pine, and stopped
To quench the thirst that, with excessive heat
And great fatigue, had robbed him of his breath.
He gazed upon the fountain which the tree
Encircled with its reins and, kneeling down,
Prepared himself to drink a pleasant draft.
But in the limpid waters he perceived
Reflected nose and mouth and cheeks and eyes.
The sight dismayed him, and he found himself
By his own loveliness betrayed; for there
He saw the image of a comely youth.
Love knew how best to avenge the stubbornness
And pride Narcissus had displayed to him.
Well was he then requited, for the youth,
Enraptured, gazed upon the crystal spring
Until he fell in love with his own face;
And at the last he died for very woe.
That was the end of that; for when he knew
Such passion must go e'er unsatisfied,
Although he was entangled in Love's snare,
And that he never could sure comfort find
In any fashion or by any means,
He lost his reason in but little space,
For very ire, and died. And so he got
The just reward that he had merited
For his refusal of a maiden's love.
You ladies, who refuse to satisfy
Your lovers, this one's case should take to heart;
For, if you let your loyal sweethearts die,
God will know how to give you recompense.

PENTHEUS

Euripides' *Bacchae*

At the end of the fifth century B.C., Euripides, just before his death, completed the tragedy that partly influenced Ovid's account of Pentheus. He dramatizes a direct confrontation between Dionysus and Pentheus. The god appears to Pentheus as a Lydian stranger; Euripides has no need, accordingly, for a character like Ovid's Acoetes. Euripides makes the god somewhat sinister and horrifying in his dedication to the king's destruction, but the king has few redeeming qualities. The following is the entrance speech of Pentheus (lines 215–248, William Arrowsmith, translator). It should be compared with the speech Ovid designs for the king in III.531–563. (Note what Euripides uses instead of the Roman allusions, which Ovid adds.)

Pentheus:
I happened to be away, out of the city,
but reports reached me of some strange mischief here,
stories of our women leaving home to frisk
in mock ecstasies among the thickets on the mountain,
dancing in honor of the latest divinity,
a certain Dionysus, whoever he may be.
In their midst stand bowls brimming with wine.
And then, one by one, the women wander off
to hidden nooks where they serve the lusts of men.
Priestesses of Bacchus they claim they are,
but it's really Aphrodite they adore.
I have captured some of them; my jailers
have locked them away in the safety of our prison.
Those who run at large shall be hunted down
out of the mountains like the animals they are—
yes, my own mother Agave, and Ino
and Autonoe, the mother of Actaeon.
In no time at all I shall have them trapped
in iron nets and stop this obscene disorder.
I am also told a foreigner has come to Thebes
from Lydia, one of those charlatan magicians,
with long yellow curls smelling of perfumes,
with flushed cheeks and the spells of Aphrodite
in his eyes. His days and nights he spends
with women and girls, dangling before them the joys
of initiation in his mysteries.
But let me bring him underneath that roof
and I'll stop his pounding with his wand and tossing
his head. By god, I'll have his head cut off.
And this is the man who claims that Dionysus
is a god and was sewn into the thigh of Zeus,
when, in point of fact, that same blast of lightning
consumed him and his mother both for her lie
that she had lain with Zeus in love. Whoever
this stranger is, aren't such impostures,
such unruliness, worthy of hanging?

VOCABULARY

A

ab, ā (+ *abl.*), from, away from
abdō, -ere (3), **-didī, -ditum,** to put away, hide
***abeō, -īre** (*irreg.*), **-iī (-īvī), -itum,** to go away, vanish
***abstrahō, -here** (3), **-xī, -ctum,** to draw away, carry off
***absum, abesse** (*irreg.*), **āfuī,** to be distant (from), absent, away
accēdō, -dere (3), **-ssī, -ssum,** to go toward, approach, be added
ācer, ācris, ācre, sharp, keen, eager
accipiō, -ipere (3), **-ēpī, -eptum,** to receive, accept
ad (+ *acc.*), toward, to, until, for
***addō, -ere** (3), **-idī, -itum,** to consider additionally, take into account as well
***addūcō, -cere** (3), **-xī, -ctum,** to draw up, wrinkle, bring to or toward
***adeō, -īre** (*irreg.*), **-iī (-īvī), -itum,** to approach
adferō, -ferre (*irreg.*), **attulī, allātum,** to bring to
adhibeō (2), to apply, employ, summon
***adhūc,** up to the present time
adimō, -imere (3), **-ēmī, -ēmptum,** to take away, remove, deprive of
aditus, -ūs (*m*), approach, entry, access
adiūrō (1), to swear to
admittō, -ere, (3), **-mīsī, -missum,** to let go, admit, permit, commit
admoneō (2), to give warning to
***admoveō, -movēre** (2), **-mōvī, -mōtum** (+ *dat.*), to move near
adrīdeō, -dēre (2), **-sī, -sum,** to laugh at
adsonō (1), to sound at
***adspiciō, -icere** (3), **-exī, -ectum,** to observe, look at, gaze upon
adsum, -esse (*irreg.*), **-fuī,** to be present
***adsūmō, -ere** (3), **-psī, -ptum,** to take possession of, acquire
***adtonō, -āre** (1), **-uī, -itum,** to strike with a thunderbolt, astonish
***aduncus, -a, -um,** curved, hooked
advertō, -tere (3), **-tī, -sum,** to turn to
aequō (1), to make equal, equal
***aequor, -oris** (*n*), the sea
aes, aeris (*n*), copper, bronze, brass
aestus, -ūs (*m*), heat, tide, commotion
aetās, -ātis (*f*), age, time of life
***aethēr, -eris** (*m*), heaven, the sky
***aevum, -ī** (*n*), age, length of years
ager, agrī (*m*), field, territory, land
***agitō** (1), to drive, shake, brandish
agmen, -inis (*n*), line of march, column
agō, -ere (3), **ēgī, āctum,** to do, act, drive, treat
***āiō** (*defective*), **ais, ait, āiunt,** to say
***albus, -a, -um,** white
aliquis, -quid, something, anyone, anything
aliter, otherwise
alius, -a, -ud, other, another
alō, -ere (3), **aluī, alitum (altum),** to feed, nourish, support
alter, -ra, -rum, the other (of two), the second, the next
altus, -a, -um, high, deep
amīcus, -ī (*m*), friend
***amnis, -is** (*m/f*), river, current
***amō** (1), to love
***amor, -ōris** (*m*), love, the beloved
an, or
***anima, -ae** (*f*), breath, soul
animus, -ī (*m*), mind, courage
annus, -ī (*m*), year
ante (*adverb, preposition* + *acc.*), before
***antemna, -ae** (*f*), yardarm on a ship
***antrum -ī** (*n*), cave, den
***anus, -ūs** (*f*), old woman
***aper, aprī** (*m*), boar
aperiō, -īre (4), **-uī, apertum,** to open
appellō (1), to name, call, address
***aptus, -a, -um** (+ *dat.*), useful, appropriate
aqua, -ae (*f*), water
arbor, -oris (*f*), tree
aridus, -a, -um, dry, arid, thirsty
arma, -ōrum (*n pl*), arms
***ars, -tis** (*f*), skill, art, method
***arvum, -ī** (*n*), ploughed field, (pl.) territory, country
at, but
atque, ac, and
attenuō (1), to make thin
attrahō, -here (3), **-xī, -ctum,** to draw to
audāx, -ācis, bold daring
audiō (4), to hear
***auferō, -rre** (*irreg.*), **abstulī, ablātum,** to take away
***augur, -uris** (*m*), prophet of bird signs
***aura, -ae** (*f*), air, breeze
***auris, -is** (*f*), ear
***aurum, -ī** (*n*), gold

aut, or
aut . . . aut, either . . . or
***autumnālis, -is, -e,** of autumn, autumnal

B

***baculum, -ī** (*n*), walking stick
***barba, -ae** (*f*), beard
***bellicus, -a, -um,** warlike, of war
bellum, -ī (*n*), war
bene, well
***bibō, -ere** (3), **-ī,** to drink
bicolor, -ōris, of two colors
bonus, -a, -um, good
***brācchium, -ī** (*n*), arm
brevis, -is, -e, short, low, brief

C

***cacūmen, -inis** (*n*), peak, top
caedēs, -is (*f*), slaughter, massacre
***caelō** (1), to emboss, engrave
***caelum, -ī** (*n*), sky
***caerul(e)us, -a, -um,** blue, blue-green
campus, -ī (*m*), plain
***candidus, -a, -um,** white, clear
***candor, -ōris** (*m*), whiteness
***canna, -ae** (*f*), reed
***capella, -ae** (*f*), she-goat
***capillus, -ī** (*m*), hair
capiō, -ere (3), **cēpī, -tum,** to take, assume, catch, seize
***captō** (1), to chase, try to catch
caput, -itis (*n*), head
***carīna, -ae** (*f*), keel, hull, ship
***casa, -ae** (*f*), hut, cottage
cāsus, -ūs (*m*), chance, accident
***cavus, -a, -um,** hollow, concave, porous
celer, -eris, -ere, swift
centum, a hundred
***cēra, -ae** (*f*), wax
cernō, -ere (3), **crēvī, crētum**, to see, distinguish, discern
***certē**, certainly, without any doubt
***cervus, -ī** (*m*), stag
cēterus, -a, -um, the rest of, the other
***cingō, -gere** (3), **-xī, -ctum,** to encircle, surround
***circā** (+ *acc.*), round, near, about
circumdō, -are (1), **-edī, -atum,** to put around, surround
circumfluō, -ere (3), **-xī**, to flow around
circumstō, -āre (1), **-etī**, to stand around
***citus, -a, -um,** quick, speedy
clāmō (1), to shout
***clāmor, -ōris** (*m*), shout, shouting, roar
***clārus, -a, -um,** loud, clear
claudō, -dere (3), **-sī, -sum,** to close
***clīvus, -ī** (*m*), slope, incline
***coeō, -īre** (*irreg.*), **-iī (-īvī), -itum,** to meet, come together
coepī, -isse (*defective*), **-tum**, to have begun
cōgō, -ere (3), **coēgī, coāctum,** to round up, assemble, collect, compel
colligō, -igere (3), **-ēgī, -ēctum,** to collect, gather
collis, -is (*m*), hill
***collum, -ī** (*n*), neck
***colō, -ere** (3), **-uī, cultum,** to inhabit, till, farm, look after, worship
***color, -ōris** (*m*), color, pigment
columna, -ae (*f*), column, pillar
***comes, -itis** (*m*), companion, friend
commūnis, -is, -e, common
***concors, -dis,** like-minded, harmonious
***coniunx, -ugis** (*m/f*), husband or wife
conplexus, -ūs (*m*), embrace
***conpōnō, -ōnere** (3), **-osuī, -ositum**, to arrange, compose
cōnspiciō, -ere (3), **-spexī, -spectum**, to see, catch sight of
cōnsuēscō, -ere (3), **-suēvī, -suētum**, to become accustomed, (perfect) be accustomed
cōnsulō, -ere (3), **-uī, -tum**, to plan, consult
contemnō, -ere (3), **-tempsī, -temptum**, to despise, scorn
***contemptor, -ōris** (*m*), despiser, scorner
***contingō, -ingere** (3), **-igī, -āctum** (+ *dat.*), to fall to one's lot, touch
cōpia, -ae (*f*), plentiful supply, abundance, (pl.) forces, troops
cornū, -ūs (*n*), horn, wing of an army
***cornum, -ī** (*n*), wild cherry
***corpus, -oris** (*n*), body, corpse
***crātēr, -ēris** (*m*), mixing bowl for wine
crēdō, -ere (3), **-idī, -itum** (+ *dat.*), to entrust, believe, credit
***crēscō, -ere** (3), **crēvī, crētum,** to arise, be born, increase
***crīnis, -is** (*m*), hair
***crūdēlis, -is, -e,** cruel
***cruor, -ōris** (*m*), blood, slaughter
cum (+ *abl.*), with, together with
cum, when, since, although
***cūnctus, -a, -um,** the whole of, all
***cupīdō, -inis** (*m/f*), longing, desire
cupiō, -ere (3), **-īvī (-iī), -ītum,** to desire, want
cūr, why
cūra, -ae (*f*), anxiety, care
currō, -ere (3), **cucurrī, cursum**, to run
cursus, -ūs (*m*), running, race, course
custodia, -ae (*f*), protection, defense
***cutis, -is** (*f*), skin

D

***damnō** (1), to condemn, reject
dē (+ *abl.*), down from, away from
dēbeō, (2), to owe, ought
***decet, -ēre** (2), **-uit** (*impersonal*), to add grace to, adorn
***dēcipiō, -ipere** (3), **-ēpī, -eptum,** to deceive, cheat

dēcurrō, -rrere (3), **-cucurrī, -cursum**, to run down from
decus, -ōris (*n*), distinction, glory, handsome face
***dēdūcō, -cere** (3), **-xī, -ctum,** to lead away, remove, draw out
dēferō, -rre (*irreg.*), **dētulī, dēlātum,** to carry down or away, report, entrust
***dēmō, -ere** (3), **-psī, -ptum,** to remove, take away
***dēnique,** finally, at last, in short
dēnsus, -a, -um, dense, thick
***dēprendō, -dere** (3), **-dī, -sum,** to catch, seize
***dēserō, -ere** (3), **-uī, -tum,** to forsake, leave, desert, fail
dēsiliō, -īre (4), **-uī, -ultum**, to jump down
dēspiciō, -icere (3), **-exī, -ectum,** to look down on, disdain, despise
dēsum, -esse (*irreg.*), **-fuī, -futūrus**, to fail, be lacking
deus, -ī (*m*), god
dexter, -(e)ra, -(e)rum, right(hand), favorable
dīcō, -ere (3), **dīxī, dictum,** to say, speak, tell
***dictum, -ī** (*n*), what is said, word
***dignor, -ārī** (1), **-ātus sum** (+ *abl.*), to treat as worthy
dignus, -a, -um, worthy, appropriate
***dīligō, -igere** (3), **-ēxī, -ēctum,** to hold dear, love, divide
dīripiō, -ere (3), **-ripuī, -reptum**, to plunder
***dīrus, -a, -um,** awful, dire, dreadful
***discēdō, -dere** (3), **-ssī, -ssum,** to disperse, desert, give up
diū, for a long time
dīversus, -a, -um, separated, different, diverse
dīvidō, -ere (3), **dīvīsī, dīvīsum**, to divide
dō, dare (1), **dedī, datum,** to give, grant, hand over
doleō (2) (+ *dat.*), to grieve (at), ache, hurt
***dolor, -ōris** (*m*), grief, pain
***dominus, -ī** (*m*), master of a house, lord
domus, -ūs (*f*), house, home
dubitō (1), to doubt, be uncertain, wonder
dubius, -a, -um, doubtful, uncertain
dūcō, -cere (3), **-xī, -ctum,** to lead
dum, as long as, while, until, provided that
duo, -ae, -o, two
***dūrō** (1), to harden, solidify
dūrus, -a, -um, hard, solid, stubborn
dux, ducis (*m*), leader, guide

E

***ecquis, -id,** is there anyone who? is there anything that?
***ēdō, -ere** (3), **-idī, -itum,** to give out, utter, proclaim
efficiō, -ere (3), **-ēcī, -ectum,** to cause, effect, bring about
efflō (1), to blow out
ego, I
***eheu,** alas
enim, for, namely, indeed, truly
eō, īre (*irreg.*), **iī (īvī), itum**, to go
equus, -ī (*m*), horse
***ergō,** for that reason, therefore
***errō** (1), to wander, roam
***error, -ōris** (*m*), mistake, error
et, and
etiam, still, yet, also, as well, even
ēveniō, -venīre (4), **-vēnī, -ventum**, to come out
ex, ē (+ *abl.*), out of
exeō, -īre (*irreg.*), **-iī (-īvī), -itum**, to go out
exiguus, -a, -um, small, scanty
exitus, -ūs (*m*), outcome, outlet, end
exsiliō, -īre (4), **-uī, -sultum**, to jump out
exspectō (1), to wait for
extrēmus, -a, -um, outermost, last

F

faciēs, -iēī (*f*), shape, form, face
facilis, -is, -e, easy
faciō, -ere (3), **fēcī, factum,** to make, build, do
fāgus, -ī (*f*), beech (tree or wood)
***fallāx, -ācis,** deceitful, deceptive
fallō, -lere (3), **fefellī, -sum,** to deceive, be mistaken, while away
fāma, -ae (*f*), news, rumor, tradition, reputation, fame
***famulus, -ī** (*m*), servant, slave
***fateor, -ērī** (2), **fassus sum,** to accept as true, acknowledge
***fātum, -ī** (*n*), destiny, fate, death
***faveō, -ēre** (2), **fāvī, fautum** (+ *dat.*), to approve of, show favor to
***fax, -cis** (*f*), torch, wedding torch, torch material
fēmina, -ae (*f*), woman
ferē, almost, approximately, usually
feritās, -ātis (*f*), wildness, savagery
ferō, ferre (*irreg.*), **tulī, lātum**, to bring, carry, bear, endure
ferrum, -ī (*n*), iron, steel, sword
ferus, -a, -um, wild, uncultivated, uncivilized
***ferveō, -ēre** (2), **ferbuī,** to boil, seethe
***fessus, -a, -um,** tired, weary, exhausted
***fēstus, -a, -um,** festive, holiday
fidēs, -eī (*f*), good faith, trust, assurance
fīnis, -is (*m*), boundary, end, (pl.) territory
fīō, fierī (*irreg.*), **factus sum**, to be made, be done, become, happen
***firmō** (1), to confirm
***flamma, -ae** (f), flame
***flāveō** (2), to be yellow
***flāvus, -a, -um,** yellow, fair-haired
***flectō, -ctere** (3), **-xī, -xum,** to bend, turn, guide
fleō, -ēre (2), **-ēvī, -ētum,** to cry, weep
flūmen, -inis (*n*), river, stream, current

***focus, -ī** (*m*), hearth
***folium, -ī** (*n*), leaf
***fōns, -ntis** (*f*), spring, well, source
***foris, -is** (*f*), door
fōrma, -ae (*f*), form, appearance, shape
***fōrmōsus, -a, -um,** beautiful, handsome
***forte,** by chance, as it happens
frāter, -tris (*m*), brother
***fraus, -dis** (*f*), offense, deceit, fraud
***fremō, -ere** (3), **-uī, -itum,** to roar, rumble, grumble, growl
***frequentō** (1), to populate, crowd, assemble
***frondeō,** (2), to put forth leaves
***frōns, -ndis** (*f*), foliage
frōns, -ntis (*f*), forehead, brow, front
frūstrā, in vain, to no purpose
fuga, -ae (*f*), flight
***fugāx, -ācis,** swift, apt to flee
fugiō, -ere (3), **fūgī,** to flee, escape
***fulmen, -inis** (*n*), lightning, thunderbolt
***fūnis, -is** (*m*), rope, cable
***furca, -ae** (*f*), fork, forked prop
***furō, -ere** (3), to be mad or crazed, rave
***furor, -ōris** (*m*), madness

G

***geminus, -a, -um,** twin, like, identical
gēns, gentis (*f*), tribe
genus, -eris (*n*), kind, class, race
gerō, -ere (3), **gessī, gestum,** to carry, carry on, wage (war)
glōria, -ae (*f*), fame, glory
***gradus, -ūs** (*m*), step, pace
grātus, -a, -um, pleasing, grateful
gravis, -is, -e, heavy, pregnant, serious
***grex, -egis** (*m*), flock, herd, crowd

H

habeō (2), to have
habitābilis, -is, -e, fit to live in, habitable
***haedus, -ī** (*m*), young goat, kid
***haereō, -rēre** (2), **-sī, -sum,** to adhere, cling, stick
***harundō, -inis** (*f*), reed
***haud,** not
***hauriō, -rīre** (4), **-sī (-riī), -stum,** to drink, empty out, consume
***herba, -ae** (*f*), small plant, herb, grass
hībernus, -a, -um, wintry
hic, haec, hoc, this
***hīc,** here
honor, -ōris (*m*), respect, honor
hōra, -ae (*f*), hour, the time, a season
***horreō** (2), to shudder at, dread, bristle
hortātor, -ōris (*m*), encourager
***hortus, -ī** (*m*), garden
***hospes, -itis** (*m*), guest, visitor, (as adjective) foreign, alien
hūc, hither, to this point
humilis, -is, -e, low, short, humble, lowly

I

***iaceō** (2), to lie, rest
***iactō** (1), to toss, hurl
iam, now, by now
īdem, eadem, idem, the same
ignis, -is (*m*), fire
ille, illa, illud, that
***illīc,** there
***imāgō, -inis** (*f*), reflection, image
imperō (1), to command, order
in (+ *abl.*), in, on
in (+ *acc.*), into, against
***inānis, -is, -e,** empty, hollow, deserted
incipiō, -ipere (3), **-ēpī, -eptum,** to start, begin
incitō (1), to incite, rouse
inde, from that place, from there
īnferō, -ferre (*irreg.*), **-tulī, illātum,** to bring in
***ingēns, -ntis,** huge, vast
inīquus, -a, -um, uneven, unfair, unfavorable
***inmēnsus, -a, -um,** boundless, huge
***inmītis, -is, -e,** harsh, merciless
inmōbilis, -is, -e, immovable, fixed
***inpius, -a, -um,** godless, undutiful, disloyal
inpleō, -ēre (2), **-ēvī, -ētum,** to fill, fill up
inpōnō, -ōnere (3), **-osuī, -ositum,** to put in or on, (perfect participle) situated
***inquit** (*from* **inquam**), he says
***īnsānia, -ae** (*f*), madness
intābēscō, -ēscere (3), **-uī,** to waste away
inter (+ *acc.*), between, among
intereā, meanwhile, in the meantime
intrā (+ *acc.*), within, inside of
inveniō, -enīre (4), **-ēnī, -entum,** to meet, find, discover
***io** (*interjection*), ho
ipse, -a, -um, -self
***īra, -ae** (*f*), anger, rage
***īrātus, -a, -um,** angry, enraged
is, ea, id, this, that, he, she, it
iste, ista, istud, this, that (of yours)
***iterum,** again, for the second time
iubeō, -bēre (2), **-ssī, -ssum,** to order (someone to do something)
iungō, -gere (3), **-xī, -ctum,** to harness, yoke, join, connect
iūrō (1), to swear, take an oath
iūs, iūris (*n*), right, law
iūstus, -a, -um, lawful, rightful, fair, just
***iuvenālis, -is, -e,** youthful, young
iuvenca, -ae (*f*), young cow, heifer
***iuvencus, -ī** (*m*), young bull, bullock
***iuvenis, -is** (*m*), young man
iuvō, -āre (1), **iūvī, iūtum,** to help

L

***lābor, -bī** (3), **-psus sum,** to glide, slip, flow, sink
labor, -ōris (*m*), work, labor, hardship

labōrō (1), to toil, struggle, suffer
*__lac, lactis__ (*n*), milk
*__lac coāctum,__ cheese
*__lacertus, -ī__ (*m*), upper arm
*__lacrima, -ae__ (*f*), tear, (pl.) weeping
*__lacus, -ūs__ (*m*), lake, pond, pool
*__lāniger, -era, -erum,__ wool-bearing, fleecy
*__lascīvus, -a, -um,__ playful, frisky
*__lateō__ (2), to hide, lie low, take refuge
lātus, -a, -um, broad, wide
laudō (1), to praise
laus, laudis (*f*), praise
lēnis, -is, -e, mild, gentle
*__lētum, -ī__ (*n*), death
levis, -is, -e, light, nimble, slight
*__lēvis, -is, -e,__ smooth, slippery
leviter, lightly, gently
*__levō__ (1), to lift, remove
licet, -ēre (2), **-uit (-itum est)** (*impersonal*), it is permitted, one may
*__liquefaciō, -facere__ (3), **-fēcī, -factum,** to melt, dissolve, turn to liquid
*__liquidus, -a, -um,__ liquid, fluid
lītus, -oris (*n*), seashore, coast, beach
locus, -ī (*m*), place, spot, position
longus, -a, -um, long
loquor, -ī (3), **locūtus sum,** to talk, speak, say
lūcidus, -a, -um, bright, clear
*__lūdō, -dere__ (3), **-sī, -sum,** to play, have fun, trick
*__lūmen, -inis__ (*n*), light, eye
*__luō, -ere__ (3), **-ī,** to suffer (a punishment), pay a penalty
lūx, lūcis (*f*), light

M

magis, more, rather
magnus, -a, -um (*comparative* **maior, maius,** *superlative* **maximus, -a, -um**), large, great
malus, -a, -um, bad, unpleasant, harmful
  male, badly, ill
maneō, -ēre (2), **-sī, -sum,** to remain, stay, continue
*__mānēs, -ium__ (*m pl*), the spirits of the dead
manus, -ūs (*f*), hand
mare, -is (*n*), the sea
*__marmor, -oris__ (*n*), marble
māter, -tris (*f*), mother
*__mātūrus, -a, -um,__ ripe, full-grown, mature
mē, me
medius, -a, -um, central, middle, medium
*__membrum, -ī__ (*n*), limb
*__memor, -oris,__ mindful, remembering
mēns, -tis (*f*), mind
*__mēnsa, -ae__ (*f*), table
mereō (2), to earn, win, gain, deserve
*__mergō, -gere__ (3), **-sī, -sum,** to sink, drown, flood, dip, immerse
*__merum, -ī__ (*n*), pure wine
metus, -ūs (*m*), fear, dread, anxiety

meus, -a, -um, my, mine
mihi, to me
mīlle (*indeclinable*), a thousand
minuō, -ere (3), **-uī, -ūtum**, to diminish, lessen, make smaller
mīror, -ārī (1), **-ātus sum**, to wonder at, be surprised
mīrus, -a, -um, strange, wonderful
*__misceō, -ēre__ (2), **-uī, mixtum,** to mix, bring together
miser, -era, -erum, poor, wretched
*__miserābilis, -is, -e,__ wretched
mittō, -ere (3), **mīsī, missum,** to send, utter, release
*__moderāmen, -inis__ (*n*), control, restraint, rudder
modo, just, only,
  nōn modo . . . sed etiam, not only . . . but also
*__moenia, -ium__ (*n pl*), defensive walls of a town, fortified town
*__mōles, -is__ (*f*), large mass, lump, pile
*__mollis, -is, -e,__ soft, loose, pliant
moneō (2), to warn, remind (of), advise
mōns, montis (*m*), mountain, hill
mora, -ae (*f*), delay
*__morior, -ī__ (3), **-tuus sum**, to die, wither
mors, -tis (*f*), death, annihilation
*__mortālis, -is, -e,__ mortal, human
mōs, mōris (*m*), custom, habit
mōtus, -ūs (*m*), movement, revolt
moveō, -ēre (2), **mōvī, mōtum,** to move
multus, -a, -um, much, (pl.)many
mūnus, -eris (*n*), task, duty, tribute, present, favor

N

nam, certainly, for, moreover
namque, for indeed, for
*__nāris, -is__ (*f*), nose, (pl.) nostrils
nārrō (1), to relate, describe, tell
nāscor, -ī (3), **nātus sum**, to be born, come into being
nātūra, -ae (*f*), nature
*__nauta, -ae__ (*m*), sailor, seaman
nē, that . . . not, lest, that
-ne, interrogative particle
necō (1), to kill
negō (1), to say . . . not, deny
neque, nec, and . . . not, neither, nor
  neque . . . neque, neither . . . nor
*__nesciō__ (4), not to know
neu, and . . . not, nor
*__niger, -gra, -grum,__ black, dark-colored
nigrēscō, -ere (3), **-gruī**, to grow black
nihil, nīl (*n indeclinable*), nothing
nisi, unless, if . . . not
*__nitidus, -a, -um,__ bright, radiant
*__nītor, -tī__ (3), **-xus (-sus) sum**, to lean on, support oneself, strain, make an effort
*__niveus, -a, -um,__ snowy, snow-white

nōbilis, -is, -e, prominent, well-known
nōbīs, to us, by us
noceō (2), to harm, injure
nōlō, nōlle (*irreg.*), **nōluī**, to be unwilling, not wish
nōmen, -inis (*n*), name
nōn, not
nōndum, not yet
nōs, we, us
nōscō, -ere (3), **nōvī, nōtum**, to become acquainted with, (perfect) know
noster, -tra, -trum, our, ours
***notō** (1), to mark, take note of
***novissimus, -a, -um**, most recent, latest
***novitās, -ātis** (*f*), surprise, novelty
novus, -a, -um, new
nox, noctis (*f*), night
nūllus, -a, -um, no, not one
***nūmen, -inis** (*n*), divine or supernatural power, divinity, divine presence
numerus, -ī (*m*), number
nunc, now
***nusquam**, in no place, nowhere
***nūtus, -ūs** (*m*), nod (of the head)
***nympha, -ae** (*f*), nymph, a semi-divine female spirit inhabiting woods, waters, etc.

O

***obstipēscō, -ēscere** (3), **-uī**, to be struck dumb, be stunned
***obstō, -āre** (1), **-itī, -ātum** (+ *dat.*), to stand in the way of, hinder
oculus, -ī (*m*), eye
omnis, -is, -e, all, the whole of
***opācus, -a, -um**, shady, dark
opportūnus, -a, -um, favorable, opportune
ops, opis (*f*), aid, (pl.) power, resources, wealth
opus, -eris (*n*), work
***ōra, -ae** (*f*), edge, boundary, shore
orior, -īrī (4), **ortus sum**, to rise, arise
***ōs, ōris** (*n*), mouth, lips, face
os, ossis (*n*), bone
***ōsculum, -ī** (*n*), kiss, mouth
ostendō, -dere (3), **-dī, -tum** (**-sum**), to show, reveal, point out
***ovīle, -is** (*n*), pen for sheep, sheepfold

P

***palma, -ae** (*f*), palm tree, date, palm (of the hand)
palūs, -ūdis (*f*), marsh, swamp
***paluster, -tris, -tre**, marshy, swampy
pār, paris, equal, level, similar
***pār, paris** (*n*), a pair
parēns, -ntis (*m*), a parent, ancestor
parō (1), to provide, produce, prepare
pars, -tis (*f*), part, role, direction, side
parte (*ablative of respect*), in part, partly
parvus, -a, -um (*comparative* **minor, minus**, *superlative* **minimus, -a, -um**), small, little
passus, -ūs (*m*), pace
pateō, -ēre (2), **patuī**, to extend, be open
pater, -tris (*m*), father
patior, patī (3), **passus sum**, to allow, permit, suffer
***patria, -ae** (*f*), one's native land
***patulus, -a, -um**, broad, wide open
paucī, -ae, -a, few
paulātim, little by little, gradually
paulum, a little, for a short while or distance
***pauper, -eris**, poor, meager, of little worth
***pectus, -oris** (*n*), breast
***pecus, -dis** (*f*), any farm animal (especially sheep)
pecus, -oris (*n*), livestock, especially sheep and cattle
pellō, -ere (3), **pepulī, pulsum**, to drive, rout
***Penātēs, -ium** (*m pl*), the gods of a Roman household, one's home
***pendeō, -ēre** (2), **pependī**, to hang, be suspended
***penna (pinna), -ae** (*f*), feather, wing, fin
per (+ *acc.*), through
***percutiō, -tere** (3), **-ssī, -ssum**, to strike
***perdō, -ere** (3), **-idī, -itum**, to ruin, destroy, lose, fail
pereō, -īre (*irreg.*), **-iī (-īvī), -itum**, to perish, be spent
***perstō, -āre** (1), **-itī, -ātum**, to persist
***perveniō, -enīre** (4), **-ēnī, -entum**, to get to, land on, reach
pēs, pedis (*m*), foot
petō -ere (3), **-īvī (-iī), -ītum**, to aim at, seek, solicit, beg
***pingō, -ngere** (3), **-nxī, -ctum**, to paint
***pīnus, -ūs** (*f*), pine (tree or wood), a ship made of pine
placeō, -ēre (2), **-uī (-itum)**, to please
***plangō, -ere** (3), **-xī, -ctum**, to beat one's breast
***plūma, -ae** (*f*), feather
poena, -ae (*f*), penalty, punishment
***pōmum, -ī** (*n*), fruit tree, fruit
pōnō, pōnere (3), **posuī, positum**, to place, put, take off
***pontus, -ī** (*m*), the sea
***porrigō, -igere** (3), **-exī, -ectum**, to extend, offer
porta, -ae (*f*), gate of a city or town
portus, -ūs (*m*), harbor, port, haven
poscō, -ere (3), **poposcī**, to demand
possum, posse (*irreg.*), **potuī**, to be able, can
post (+ *acc.*), after, behind
postquam, after, when, ever since
***potentia, -ae** (*f*), power, influence, rule
potestās, -ātis (*f*), power, chance, possibility
praebeō (2), to show, offer, present, supply
praeda, -ae (*f*), booty, prey, reward
praesēns, -ntis, present, in person, ready
praeter (+ *acc.*), beyond, besides, except
***precor, -ārī** (1), **-ātus sum**, to ask or pray for something

prex, -ecis (*f*), prayer, entreaty, curse
prīmus, -a, -um, first
prīmō, first, at first
prior, -ius, former
prō (+ *abl.*), before, for, in behalf of
probō (1), to approve of, test, prove
***prōcērus, -a, -um,** tall, lofty
procul, far away, at a distance
prohibeō, (2), to keep at a distance, prevent, protect
***prōlēs, -is** (*f*), offspring
***promineō** (2), to project, stick out
***prōmittō, -ittere** (3), **-īsī, -issum,** to promise
***propior, -ior, -ius,** nearer, closer
prospectō (1), to look forth at
***prōspiciō, -icere** (3), **-exī, -ectum,** to see before one
prōtinus, at once
prōturbō (1), to drive forward
prūdēns, -entis, wise, foreseeing
***prūnum, -ī** (*n*), plum
***puella, -ae** (*f*), girl
puer, -erī (*m*), boy
pugna, -ae (*f*), fight
***pulcher, -chra, -chrum,** beautiful, handsome
***puppis, -is** (*f*), stern of a boat, ship
***purpureus, -a, -um,** purple
putō (1), to ponder, think

Q

quaerō, -ere (3), **-s(i)ī (-sīvī), -sītum,** to search for, seek, ask for
***quamvīs,** although
quantus, -a, -um, how great, how much, (as great) as
-que, and
***quercus, -ūs** (*f*), oak
queror, -rī (3), **-stus sum,** to complain
quī, quae, quod, who, which, that, which? what?
quidem, indeed, certainly
quiēs, -ētis (*f*), quiet
quis, quid, who? what? which?
quisquam, quicquam (quidquam), anyone, anything
***quisquis, quaequae, quidquid (quicquid),** whoever, whatever
***quondam**, formerly
quoniam, since
quoque, also
***quot** (*indeclinable*), how many
quot . . . tot, as many . . . so many
***quotiēns,** how often? as often as

R

***rāmus, -ī** (*m*), branch
rapiō, -ere (3), **-uī, -tum,** to seize, snatch, carry off
recēns, -ntis, recent, fresh
***recipiō, -ipere** (3), **-ēpī, -eptum,** to receive, welcome

reddō, -ere (3), **-idī, -itum,** to give back, restore, reply
redeō, -īre (4), **-iī (-īvī), -itum,** to go back, return
***referō, -rre** (*irreg.*), **rettulī, relātum,** to bring back, reply
refugiō, -ugere (3), **-ūgī,** to flee back
***rēgnō** (1), to rule as king, reign
rēgnum, -ī (*n*), royal power, monarchy, realm
relinquō, -inquere (3), **-īquī, -ictum,** to leave, forsake, abandon
***remaneō, -ēre** (2), **-sī,** to remain, stay behind
remittō, -ittere (3), **-īsī, -issum,** to send back, release, relax
rēmus, -ī (*m*), oar
***repellō, -ere** (3), **reppulī, repulsum,** to push or drive away, rebuff
repetō, -ere (3), **-īvī (-iī), -ītum**, to seek again
repleō, -ēre (2), **-ēvī, -ētum**, to refill, replenish
reportō (1), to carry back
***requiēs, -ētis** (*f*), rest, repose
rēs, reī (*f*), thing, matter, affair
resiliō, -īre (4), **-uī, -ultum**, to jump back
respondeō, -dēre (2), **-dī, -sum,** to reply, answer
***restō, -āre** (1), **-itī,** to withstand, oppose
reticeō (2), to keep silent
***retineō, -ēre** (2), **-uī, retentum,** to hold fast, detain, stop
revertor, -vertī (3), **-versus sum,** to return, go back
***rīdeō, -dēre** (3), **-sī, -sum,** to laugh, laugh at
***rigidus, -a, -um,** rigid, stiff
***riguus, -a, -um,** irrigated, well-watered
rogō (1), to ask, ask for
***rubor, -ōris** (*m*), redness, blush
***ruō, -ere** (3), **-ī,** to rush, collapse
rūrsus, backwards, once again

S

***sacer, -cra, -crum,** sacred, holy
saepe, often
***saeta, -ae** (*f*), coarse or stiff animal hair
***saevus, -a, -um,** savage, ferocious
sagitta, -ae (*f*), arrow
***salignus, -a, -um,** made of willow wood
***saltus, -ūs** (*m*), woodland, glade
***saltus, -ūs** (*m*), jump, leap
salūs, -ūtis (*f*), safety
***Saturnius, -a, -um,** of Saturn, Saturn's
saxum, -ī (*n*), rock, stone
sciō (4), to know
***scopulus, -ī** (*m*), rock, boulder
sē, (by) himself, herself, itself, themselves
***secō, -āre** (1), **-uī, -tum,** to cut, carve, detach
sed, but
***sēdēs, -is** (*f*), seat
***sēdūcō, -cere** (3), **-xī, -ctum,** to draw away, separate

semper, always, all the time
***senecta, -ae** (*f*), old age
***senex, -is** (*m*), an old man
senior, -ius, older
sentiō, -tīre (4), **-sī, -sum,** to feel, perceive, think
sequor, -ī (3), **secūtus sum,** to go after or behind, follow
***sermō, -ōnis** (*m*), speech, talk
servō (1), to guard, keep, save
sī, if
sibi, to himself, herself, itself, themselves
sīc, so, thus
***siccus, -a, -um,** dry
***sīdus, -eris** (*n*), star, planet
signum, -ī (*n*), mark, sign, standard
silva, -ae (*f*), wood, forest
similis, -is, -e, like, similar
simul, at the same time
***simulācrum, -ī** (*n*), a likeness, image, reflection
sine (+ *abl.*), without
***sinō, sinere** (3), **sīvī (siī), situm,** to leave alone, allow
***sistō, -ere** (3), **stetī (stitī), statum,** to stand, set, place
***sitis, -is** (*f*), thirst
sīve . . . sīve, whether . . . or
socius, -ī (*m*), companion, colleague
sōl, sōlis (*m*), the sun
***soleō, -ēre** (2), **-itus sum** (+ *infinitive*), to be accustomed
sōlus, -a, -um, alone, lonely
sōlum, only
***solvō, -vere** (3), **-vī, -ūtum,** to loosen, weaken
***sonō, -āre** (1), **-uī, -itum,** to make a noise, sound, resound
***sonus, -ī** (*m*), sound
***soror, -ōris** (*f*), sister
***spargō, -gere** (3), **-sī, -sum,** to scatter, sprinkle
spatium, -ī (*n*), distance (of space or time)
speciēs, -ēī (*f*), appearance, sight
spectō (1), to look at, watch
***spernō, -ere** (3), **sprēvī, sprētum,** to reject scornfully, spurn
spērō (1), to hope, hope for
spēs, -eī (*f*), hope, expectation
sponte (*fem. abl. sing.*), of one's own accord
stō, stāre (1), **stetī, statum**, to stand
***studium, -ī** (*n*), zeal, ardor, pursuit
***Stygius, -a, -um,** Stygian, of the Styx, a river of the underworld
sub (+ *acc.* or *abl.*), under
***subeō, -īre** (*irreg.*), **-iī (-īvī), -itum,** to succeed to, replace
subitō, suddenly
***submittō, -ittere** (3), **-īsī, -issum,** to lower, bow, bend
***sūcus, -ī** (*m*), juice, sap, moisture
sum, esse (*irreg.*), **fuī, futūrus**, to be
summus, -a, -um, highest, topmost
sūmō, -ere (3), **sūmpsī, sūmptum**, to take, assume
super (+ *acc.*), over, above, on top of
superō (1), to conquer, surpass
***superus, -a, -um,** above, higher, (pl.) the gods above
***surgō, -rgere** (3), **-rrēxī, -rrēctum,** to rise to one's feet, get up
***sūs, suis** (*m/f*), pig
suspendō, -dere (3), **-dī, -sum,** to hang, suspend
suspicor, -ārī (1), **-ātus sum**, to suspect
suus, -a, -um, his (own), her (own), its (own), their (own)

T

***tālis, -is, -e,** of such a character or kind
tam, so, so much
tamen, nevertheless
tangō, -ere (3), **tetigī, tāctum,** to touch, reach
tantus, -a, -um, so great, so much
tantum, only
tardus, -a, -um, slow
tē, you
***tēctum, -ī** (*n*), roof, ceiling
tegō, -gere (3), **-xī, -ctum,** to cover, clothe, protect
***tellūs, -ūris** (*f*), ground, earth
tēlum, -ī (*n*), missile, weapon
***templum, -ī** (*n*), temple, shrine
temptō (1), to test, try
tempus, -oris (*n*), time, season, (pl.) temples (of the head)
tendō, -ere (3), **tetendī, tentum (tēnsum),** to stretch
***tenebrae, -ārum** (*f pl*), darkness
teneō, -ēre (2), **-uī, -tum,** to hold, grasp, keep
***tener, -era, -erum,** tender, delicate
***tenuō** (1), to make thin, weaken
***tepidus, -a, -um,** warm
tergum, -ī (*n*), back, rear
terra, -ae (*f*), land, earth
terreō (2), to terrorize, alarm, terrify
terribilis, -is, -e, frightening, terrible
tertius, -a, -um, third
***thyrsus, -ī** (*m*), staff entwined with a garland and tipped with a pine cone
tibi, to you
timeō (2), to be afraid, fear
timidus, -a, -um, timid, fearful
tollō, -ere (3), **sustulī, sublātum**, to lift, raise, remove
***tormentum, -ī** (*n*), war engine, sling artillery
tot (*indeclinable*), that many, so many
totidem (*indeclinable*), the same number of, as many
***totiēns,** as often, so often

tōtus, -a, -um, the whole of, all
trabs, trabis (*f*), beam, timber
trādō, -ere (3), **-idī, -itum,** to hand over, deliver, hand down
trahō, -here (3), **trāxī, trāctum,** to drag, draw, bring along
***tremō, -ere** (3), **-uī,** to tremble, quake
***trepidus, -a, -um,** fearful, anxious, trembling
***truncus, -a, -um,** mutilated, trimmed, lopped off
***truncus, -ī** (*m*), tree trunk
tū, you
tueor, -ērī (2), **tuitus (tūtus) sum,** to defend, guard
tum, then
***turba, -ae** (*f*), riot, crowd, entourage
***turbō** (1), to agitate, disturb, muddy
turpis, -is, -e, foul, ugly, shameful
***tūtēla, -ae** (*f*), guardianship, protection
tūtus, -a, -um, safe
tuus, -a, -um, your, yours
***Tyrrhēnus, -a, -um,** Tyrrhenian Greek

U

ubi (ubī), where(?), when(?)
ūllus, -a, -um, any
ulterior, -ius, farther, further
ultimus, -a, -um, farthest, last
ultrō, besides, voluntarily
***ululātus, -ūs** (*m*), howl, wailing
***umbra, -ae** (*f*), shade
umquam, ever
***unda, -ae** (*f*), a wave (of the sea, etc.)
undique, from all sides, on all sides
***ūnicus, -a, -um,** one and only, sole, singular, outstanding
ūnus, -a, -um, one, alone
urbs, -bis (*f*), city, Rome
***ūrō, -ere** (3), **ussī, ustum,** to burn, inflame
***ursa, -ae** (*f*), she-bear
ūsus, -ūs (*m*), use, means, practice, experience
ut, that, as, when
uterque, utraque, utrumque, each (of two), both
utinam, would that, if only
***ūva, -ae** (*f*), bunch of grapes

V

vacuus, -a, -um, empty
vagor, -ārī (1), **-ātus sum,** to wander
valeō (2), to be strong
valē, good-bye
vallēs (vallis), -is (*f*), valley
***vānus, -a, -um,** false, unreliable
***vātēs, -is** (*m*), prophet, seer
***-ve** (*enclitic conjunction*), or
***vēlō** (1), to cover, clothe, conceal
***vēlum, -ī** (*n*), sail
***venia, -ae** (*f*), favor, kindness, pardon
veniō, venīre (4), **vēnī, ventum,** to come
ventus, -ī (*m*), wind
***verbum, -ī** (*n*), word
vertō, -tere (3), **-tī, -sum,** to turn, turn up, overturn
vērus, -a, -um, real, true
vester, -tra, -trum, your, yours
***vestīgium, -ī** (*n*), footprint, sole of the foot
vestis, -is (*f*), dress, clothing
***vetō, -āre** (1), **-uī, -itum,** to forbid
vetus, -eris, old
via, -ae (*f*), road, channel, journey
***vīcīnus, -a, -um,** neighboring
videō, -ēre (2), **vīdī, vīsum,** to see
vincō, -ere (3), **vīcī, victum,** to conquer, overcome
***vīnum, -ī** (*n*), wine
***violentus, -a, -um,** violent, savage, aggressive
***violō** (1), to violate, profane, dishonor
vir, virī (*m*), man, husband
vīs, vīs (*f*) (*pl* **vīrēs, vīrium**), strength, force
vīta, -ae (*f*), life
***vītis, -is** (*f*), grapevine
vīvō, -vere (3), **-xī, -ctum,** to live, live on, survive
vīvus, -a, -um, living, alive
vix, hardly, scarcely
vōbīs, to you, by you (pl.)
vocō (1), to call, call upon, summon
volō, velle (*irreg.*), **voluī,** to wish, be willing
***volucer, -cris, -cre,** flying, swift
voluntās, -ātis (*f*), wish, good-will
vōs, you (pl.)
***vōtum, -ī** (*n*), vow, prayer, desire
vōx, vōcis (*f*), voice, utterance, speech
vulnus, -eris (*n*), wound
***vultus, -ūs** (*m*), face, countenance